The basics of international law

Manchester University Press

The basics of international law

The UK context

Math Noortmann
and Luke D. Graham

Manchester University Press

The right of Math Noortmann and Luke D. Graham to be identified as the authors of this work has been asserted in accordance with the Copyright, Designs and Patents Act 1988.

Published by Manchester University Press
Oxford Road, Manchester M13 9PL
www.manchesteruniversitypress.co.uk

British Library Cataloguing-in-Publication Data
A catalogue record for this book is available from the British Library

ISBN 978 1 5261 6891 7 paperback

First published 2022

Typeset by Newgen Publishing UK
Printed in Great Britain by CPI Group (UK) Ltd, Croydon

Contents

Contents

Contents

Contents

Contents

Contents

Contents

Contents

Figures

Tables

Abbreviations

ANC	African National Congress
ASEAN	Association of Southeast Asian Nations
AU	African Union
Benelux	Belgium, the Netherlands, and Luxembourg
CEDAW	Convention on the Elimination of All Forms of Discrimination Against Women
CoE	Council of Europe
CPIUN	Convention on Privileges and Immunities of the United Nations
CRC	Convention on the Rights of the Child
DSB	Dispute Settlement Body (WTO)
DSU	Dispute Settlement Understanding (WTO)
ECOSOC	UN Economic and Social Council
ECOWAS	Economic Community of West African States
EEZ	Exclusive Economic Zone

List of abbreviations

EU	European Union
GATT	General Agreement on Tariffs and Trade
GEF	Global Environment Facility
HCNM	High Commissioner on National Minorities (OSCE)
IBRD	International Bank for Reconstruction and Development
ICAO	International Civil Aviation Organization
ICC	International Criminal Court
ICCPR	International Covenant on Civil and Political Rights
ICERD	International Convention on the Elimination of All Forms of Racial Discrimination
ICESCR	International Covenant on Economic, Social and Cultural Rights
ICJ	International Court of Justice
ICRC	International Committee of the Red Cross
ICSID	International Centre for the Settlement of Investment Disputes
IDA	International Development Association
IFC	International Finance Corporation
IGO	International Governmental Organisation
ILO	International Labour Organization
IMO	International Maritime Organization
IMF	International Monetary Fund

List of abbreviations

INTERPOL	International Criminal Police Organization
ISCID	International Centre for the Settlement of Investment Disputes
ITLOS	International Tribunal for the Law of the Sea
MDGs	Millennium Development Goals (UN)
NAFTA	North American Free Trade Association
NATO	North Atlantic Treaty Organization
NGO	non-governmental organisation
OAS	Organization of American States
OAU	Organization of African Unity
OPEC	Organization of the Petroleum Exporting Countries
OSCE	Organization for Security and Co-operation in Europe
OSPAR	Convention for the Protection of the Marine Environment of the North-East Atlantic
PCA	Permanent Court of Arbitration
PLO	Palestine Liberation Organization
PNA	Palestinian National Authority
SDGs	Sustainable Development Goals
TRIPS	Agreement on Trade-Related Aspects of Intellectual Property Rights
TWAIL	Third World Approaches to International Law
UDHR	Universal Declaration of Human Rights
UN	United Nations

List of abbreviations

UNAT	United Nations Administrative Tribunal
UNCAT	United Nations Convention against Torture and Other Cruel, Inhuman or Degrading Treatment or Punishment
UNCED	United Nations Conference on Environment and Development
UNCLOS	United Nations Convention on the Law of the Sea
UNCTAD	United Nations Conference on Trade and Development
UNDP	United Nations Development Programme
UNEP	United Nations Environment Programme
UNESCO	UN Educational, Scientific and Cultural Organization
UNGA	United Nations General Assembly
UNICEF	United Nations International Children's Emergency Fund
UNODC	United Nations Office for Drugs and Crime
UNSC	United Nations Security Council
VCLT	Vienna Convention on the Law of Treaties
WEU	Western European Union
WHO	World Health Organization
WTO	World Trade Organization
WTO-CTE	WTO Committee on Trade and Environment

Chapter I

Introduction

1 Definition of public international law

Public international law is the body of law that governs the legal relations between internationally recognised legal persons (mainly states and international organisations). In literature and legislation, 'public international law' is also referred to as 'international law'.

A typical public international law activity is the conclusion of treaties between states (see section 27). These treaties may concern various matters, such as air and sea transport, taxation, extradition, human rights, extinction, and intellectual property rights. The establishment of international organisations, such as the United Nations (UN) and regional organisations (see Chapter XV), is also a characteristic act of public international law. Activities of states and international organisations can lead to responsibility, litigation, and even armed conflict. These phenomena are also part of public international law.

2 The legal nature of public international law

The international legal order has a separate legal character. International law differs from national legal systems in the following respects:

- The international legal order has no central legislative, executive, or judicial power.
- International sources of law, such as treaties, customary law, and binding decisions of international organisations, are at the centre of international legal research.
- Unilateral law enforcement (self-help) is a lawful act in response to an internationally wrongful act.
- The legal relations between states – the main legal subjects of international law – are governed by the principle of formal sovereign equality.
- International law is in principle reciprocal; it is of a contractual and customary nature.

3 Historical developments

The emergence of the modern system of public international law is closely linked to the rise of the sovereign (i.e., independent) state in the seventeenth century. In the development of public international law, several phases can be distinguished:

- The period before the Peace of Westphalia (1648). This period is characterised by incidental developments in the field of maritime and commercial law, treaty law, and immunities. There is no systematic

coherence between the different international
legal rules.

- The development phase of international law (1648–
  1850). This phase is characterised by the emergence
  and development of the 'sovereign state'. States are
  mainly concerned with the demarcation of their territory and mutual jurisdiction.
- The period of coordination (from 1850 onwards).
  This period is characterised by:
  - □ the establishment of international organisations;
  - □ the institutionalisation of international dispute
    settlement procedures; and
  - □ the codification of customary international law.
- The 'Cold War' period (1947–1991) marks a break
  with the idealism of the pre-Second World War
  period. International law becomes politicised.
  Decolonisation, postcolonialism, peace and security,
  development issues, and the environment dominate
  the international agenda.
- The period of global cooperation (1990–now). This
  cooperation is expressed in:
  - □ the strengthening of regional and international
    organisations (such as the European Union (EU),
    the African Union (AU), and the World Trade
    Organization (WTO));
  - □ the increase in the activities of the UN Security
    Council (UNSC);
  - □ the organisation of UN conferences to discuss
    global problems (such as that on the environment
    and development (UNCED)) (see section 119);

□ the increase in humanitarian actions; and
□ the cooperation between intergovernmental organisations (IGOs) and non-governmental organisations (NGOs).

4 Natural law and positivism

The development of international law is mainly determined by two major legal theories:

- The *natural law doctrine* presupposes that:
  □ the law is universal and unchangeable; and
  □ the law can be discovered from a number of religious, ethical, or logical axioms.
- The theory of *(neo)positivism*, on the other hand, assumes that:
  □ the law is made by people; and
  □ the law can differ according to time and place.

Positivism is the dominant legal theory in public international law today.

5 Alternative approaches

Three other approaches to the development of international law should also be considered.

- *Critical legal theory* points out that law is not necessarily objective, neutral, and just, but is partly determined by political, social, and economic interests. The best known of these approaches are the Marxist approach, the feminist approach, and Third World Approaches to International Law (TWAIL).

- The *policy-oriented approach* views international law as a process of authorised decision-making in which various non-state actors also participate.
- The *transnational legal process approach* sees a change in international law through an increasing interpenetration between public and private actors, cross-border events, and legal systems.

6 Sub-areas of international law

International law has several specific sub-fields:
- The *classical areas of international law* (also called the law of nations) include:
  □ the law of diplomatic relations;
  □ the law of war (humanitarian); and
  □ the law of the sea.
- The *internationalised areas of law* are mainly based on principles and rules of national law which have entered the international arena, such as:
  □ international environmental law;
  □ international economic law; and
  □ international criminal law.
- *Specialised areas of law* have evolved from the classical areas of international law, but today they form independent jurisdictions, namely:
  □ the law of international organisations;
  □ EU law;

□ the law of the WTO;
□ air and space law; and
□ human rights.

The law of international organisations
(see also Chapter XII)

This area of law covers the institutional law of IGOs. These are organisations established by and composed of states. The core rules of this jurisdiction can be found in:
- the founding treaties of the IGOs;
- the rules of procedure of the IGOs;
- specific treaties and documents on the immunity and responsibility of international organisations (see also sections 77 and 78).

Legal developments in the field of the law of international organisations point to the development of international administrative law.

The law of the European Union

EU law is a unique example of a far-reaching, independent legal arena within public international law. It is characterised as supranational law.

This area of law is often referred to as 'European law'. However, in addition to the EU, Europe has other independent IGOs, such as the Council of Europe (CoE) and the Organization for Security and Cooperation in Europe (OSCE). These organisations are typically international.

In 2020 the UK officially terminated the Treaty on European Union (1993) in accordance with Article 50 and thereby left the EU. The right of an EU Member State to unilaterally terminate the EU Treaty underlines the public international law character of this Treaty.

7 Adjacent legal fields

Adjacent legal fields are areas of law which are closely linked to – yet do not form part of – public international law.

International private law

International private law (also called conflict of laws) governs the cross-border legal relations between national legal persons. To determine the extent to which different national legal rules may apply to the same cross-border legal relationship, a national court must determine:
- which national law is applicable;
- which court has jurisdiction to apply this law; and
- where and how sentences should be enforced.

Private international law may be the subject of international treaties.

Transnational law

Transnational law is formed by:

- the increasing number of investment and peace agreements between states and non-state actors such as businesses and liberation movements; and
- judgments of tribunals such as the Permanent Court of Arbitration (PCA), the Iran–US Claims Tribunal, and the International Centre for the Settlement of Investment Disputes (ISCID) in cases between states and non-state actors.

In transnational law, public international law, private international law, and national law are no longer clearly distinguishable.

Examples of arbitration cases between individuals and companies and/or states are:

- *Patel Engineering Limited (India) v The Republic of Mozambique* (PCA Case No. 2020-21) concerning investments made for the development and operation of a rail corridor.
- *Ge Gao et al. (China) v INTERPOL* (PCA Case No. 2019-19) concerning the headquarters of the International Criminal Police Organization (INTERPOL) in France.
- *Larsen v Hawaiian Kingdom* (PCA Case No. 1999-01) concerning the application of domestic US law over the claimant's person, who is a resident in Hawaii, within the territorial jurisdiction of the Hawaiian Kingdom.

UK

For examples of arbitration cases in which the UK has been involved, see section 55.

8 The nation state and international law

The relationship between national states and international law differs depending on their respective historical development, geography, interests, and position. Thus, states can opt in and opt out of organisations and treaty arrangements according to their preferences. Most nation states are members of several international organisations and party to numerous bilateral and multilateral agreements.

The growth of international legal instruments also makes international legal disputes more likely. Therefore, we also see an increase in international arbitration and international court cases.

Chapter II

The place of international law in the national legal order

9 Direct effect

In many states international law influences the national legal order, that is, national judges can apply international law. In principle, the way in which rules of international law influence national law is determined by the national legal system. To establish the nature of the effect of international law, it must be determined whether:

- the effect is automatic. If the effect is automatic, the international law will not have to be transposed into national law by means of a national law. If it is not automatic, international law will have to be transposed into national law by a national law (the international law will have to be *transformed*);
- there is *direct effect* of rules of international law. This means that citizens can rely on provisions of international law before national courts;
- international law provisions can override national law.

Depending on the constitutional arrangements in each state, the relationship between international law and national law may be laid down, inter alia, in the constitution or in legislation.

UK

In England and Wales, international law does not have direct effect. The relationship between international law and domestic law is defined by dualism (see sections 10, 11, and 12). Even so, there is a strong presumption that domestic law can and should be read consistently with international law. For greater detail, see Lord Mance, 'International Law in the UK Supreme Court', The Supreme Court (2017).

10 Monism and dualism

There are two views on how international law affects the national legal order:
- The *monistic view* is based on:
  - □ the existence of one legal system, that is international and national law are not separate legal systems;
  - □ the impact of international legal rules – international law does not need to be transposed; and

- □ the superiority of international law – in case of conflict between international and national law, international law takes precedence.
- The *dualistic view* assumes that:
  - □ international and national law are separate legal systems;
  - □ international law must be transposed (transformed) by special national legislation; and
  - □ international law is not of a higher order – through transposition, international law is equal to national law.

11 Monism and dualism in practice

It is for each state to determine whether they adopt monism or dualism. Examples of states that are considered to be monistic are Belgium and Kyrgyzstan. Examples of systems that are considered to be predominantly dualistic are the UK as well as many other states which share a common law heritage such as, inter alia, Ghana and India. In practice, national legal systems are never purely monistic or purely dualistic but contain elements of both concepts.

UK

In the UK, domestic and international law are regarded as operating on different planes. Even despite this dualist approach, international law can be transposed into domestic law either by Parliament through legislation or by judges through the common law. This means that international law does not have a special legal status within the UK's domestic legal system.

12 Rules of international law having direct or indirect effect

International law traditionally creates rights and duties for states, but it can also create rights and duties for individuals. The question is: can individuals rely on the protection of the content of an international legal rule? This is referred to as *direct effect*. Case law has developed criteria to determine the direct effect of international rules of law. A national judge could consider:

- *the intention of the contracting parties*: it may be clear from the text of the treaty or from the history of its elaboration that the contracting parties intended it to have direct effect;
- *the nature and content of the provision*: direct effect is assumed if:
  □ the implementation and operation of the provision does not require any further action by the state; and
  □ the text is sufficiently precise to be invoked by individuals.

13 National government bodies and international law

Once a state has accepted to be bound by international law through explicit consent or practice, international law creates both rights and obligations for states. National constitutions stipulate which national bodies are involved in the establishment and application of international legal rules and which specific authority they have. In general, these national bodies would be the executive, the legislature, and the judiciary.

UK

UK government bodies

The executive

As a matter of UK constitutional law, foreign affairs and other matters relating to the international legal order are exercised under the Royal Prerogative by the executive on behalf of the Crown. The Royal Prerogative refers to a number of powers which have not been granted in a written constitution or through legislation but have instead derived from the common law.

The legislature

The case of *R (Miller) v Secretary of State for Exiting the European Union* [2017] UKSC 5 neatly summarises the relationship of the different branches of the British state in relation to international law. The UK Supreme Court recognised that generally the power to make or unmake treaties belonged solely to the executive and that both the legislature and the judiciary could not interfere. However, when the exercise of this prerogative power alters domestic law, the approval of the legislature is required.

The decision to deploy the armed forces is also a prerogative power, meaning that it is exercised by the executive. However, the UK government has acknowledged that a constitutional convention has developed whereby the House of Commons should first debate the matter. This convention is a 'soft' rule and has not always been adhered to.

The judiciary

The judiciary may incorporate international law into the common law (judge-made law) and may interpret domestic law to ensure alignment with international law. However, in situations where an Act of Parliament is explicitly contrary to international law, the judiciary are not able to challenge that legislation due to the doctrine of parliamentary sovereignty.

Chapter III

Subjects of international law

14 International legal personality

International legal personality is an international public law status that may confer certain rights and obligations.

- Based on international legal personality:
  - □ international rights and obligations can be obtained;
  - □ other international legal persons may be held liable;
  - □ international legal relations can be established.
- The ability to perform international legal acts, such as concluding treaties, is an indication of having international legal personality.
- Those with international legal personality are referred to as subjects of international law.
- Subjects of international law have incomplete or limited status if one or more of the above actions is not legally possible.

15 Forms of international legal personality

The content and extent of international legal personality may vary from one legal person to another. The following forms of international legal personality can be distinguished:

- *original legal personality*: this is granted only to states;
- *derived legal personality*: international legal personality may be derived from the original legal personality of states, as is the case, for example, with international organisations based on treaties;
- *limited legal personality*: here, the extent of the legal personality is related to the function of the legal person, as is often the case with international organisations;
- *unique legal personality*: these are the Holy See and the Sovereign Order of Malta. Whether a unique international legal personality for other non-state actors exists is still controversial.

16 States

The Montevideo Convention on the Rights and Duties of States (1933) sets out several requirements for statehood. These criteria are:

- a permanent population;
- a defined territory;
- effective governmental authority; and
- the capacity to enter into relations with other states.

The following circumstances are not relevant for determining whether or not an entity is a state:

- The size of the territory and/or population. Nauru, with 21 km² of territory and 13,000 inhabitants, is as much a state as the People's Republic of China (9,500,000 km² and 1.4 billion inhabitants).
- The temporary loss of power over the territory and the population. A state does not lose its sovereign independence after it has been illegally occupied by another state.
- Recognition by other states.

17 Recognition

In international law, the term 'recognition' has different meanings in different contexts.

Recognition of states

- A state does not have to be legally recognised by other states to qualify as a full international legal entity.
- According to the *declaratory theory*, recognition is only a confirmation of the actual existence of the state. This is the prevailing doctrine regarding recognition of states. The recognition of a state by other states is a political, rather than a legal, act.
- The *constitutive theory* makes the existence of a state dependent on an act of formal recognition by other states. This theory has been abandoned.

Recognition of governments and insurgents

The (non-)recognition of governments and rebellious movements is also a political act to approve or reject a change of government. In the case of civil war, a (too) early recognition of the insurgent movement as the legal authority can be considered as a violation of Article 2.7 of the UN Charter (i.e., as an interference in the internal affairs of a state). This is an international tort and may lead to state responsibility (see Chapter VIII).

De facto and de jure recognition

De facto recognition is the implicit recognition of a given factual situation. De facto recognition may be necessary for national and international legal relations. Non-recognition may lead to undesirable legal consequences in the national legal order.

De jure recognition will often be made explicit. It recognises the legitimacy of a situation and opens the possibility of diplomatic relations.

The different forms of recognition can be found in:
- the recognition of the Palestine Liberation Organization (PLO) based on the right to self-determination;
- the recognition of the Palestinian National Authority (PNA) based on the Oslo Agreement between Israel and the PLO; and
- the recognition of Palestine as an 'observer' non-member state of the UN by the UN General Assembly (UNGA).

18 Intergovernmental organisations

Two types of legal personality can be distinguished in intergovernmental organisations:

- *Legal personality under national law* (e.g., Article 104 of the UN Charter). It is used to perform legal acts under private law on the territory of Member States. Examples are renting buildings, hiring staff, or buying office supplies.
- *International legal personality*, which is required, among other things, for concluding treaties, conducting international proceedings and being able to claim immunities. International legal personality can be established in two ways in international organisations:
  - ☐ The founding treaty explicitly states that the organisation in question has international legal personality (e.g., Article 4 Statute of the International Criminal Court (ICC Statute)).
  - ☐ International legal personality can be (implicitly) derived from the objectives and functions of the organisations.

Example

In the Reparation for Injuries case (1949), the International Court of Justice (ICJ) concluded that the existence of international legal personality could be inferred from the UN's tasks and objectives in the area of peace and security. The UN should be considered autonomous in holding a state liable for the death of one of its staff members who was involved in monitoring an armistice agreement.

In the Advisory Opinion on the Interpretation of the Agreement of 25 March 1951 between the World Health Organization (WHO) and Egypt (1980), the ICJ concluded, based on an interpretation of the purposes and functions of the WHO, that this organisation cannot independently seek an advisory opinion from the ICJ.

19 Liberation movements

The legal personality of liberation movements is based on:
- the right to self-determination: all peoples have the right to resist colonial rule or racist oppression;
- the Geneva Conventions on the humanitarian law of war (see section 67);
- the recognition of states by concluding treaties;
- recognition by international organisations by granting observer status to liberation movements so that they can participate in meetings and gatherings of international organisations.

Example

The African National Congress (ANC) and the PLO are examples of liberation movements that once had international legal personality. Now, however, these organisations have been transformed into national political parties, or have been absorbed into other bodies, and no longer have an international legal personality.

20 New forms of international legal personality

International legal personality is no longer limited to the categories mentioned so far in Chapter III. The following entities can claim international legal personality:

- *Individuals*: their international legal personality is limited and results from:
  - □ the ability to guarantee human rights at the international level; and
  - □ the recognition of individual international criminal responsibility (see Chapter XVII).
- *Multi- or transnational undertakings*: while the international legal personality of companies is disputed, a possible recognition of international legal personality may be based on:
  - □ the internationalisation of private law contracts between states and companies – contracts are

often governed by international law because neither party wants the law of the other party to gov-
ern the contract;
□ the internationalisation of commercial conflicts
between states and companies;
□ the alleged international responsibility of companies for violations of human rights and international environmental law.

NGOs do not (yet) qualify as international legal persons. However, NGOs can acquire a special legal status
under international treaties and within international
organisations.

The International Committee of the Red Cross (ICRC)
has a special status under the Geneva Conventions of
1949 (the ICRC is co-responsible for the implementation of the Conventions) and has an observer status
within the UN (i.e., the ICRC can participate in meetings and has the right to speak but cannot vote). Other
international NGOs, such as Amnesty International
and Greenpeace, have consultative status within the
UN (Article 71 UN Charter). They have a limited right
to speak at meetings.

Chapter IV

Sources of public international law

21 The sources of international law

Rules of international law are found in the sources of public international law. These are listed in the first instance in Article 38 of the Statute of the ICJ and cover:

- international treaties;
- international custom, as evidence of a general practice accepted as law;
- general principles of law;
- judicial decisions;
- the views of legal scholars.

In addition, it is accepted by international law scholars that other sources of law exist. These other sources are:

- unilateral legal acts;
- *binding* decisions of international judicial institutions;
- *jus cogens* (legal rules to which no exception is permitted).

In practice, treaties, customary international law, and binding decisions by international judicial institutions are the main sources of law. Conflicts mainly arise between rules resulting from these different sources of law.

22 Treaties

Treaties are becoming increasingly important as a source of international rights and obligations. A written agreement often offers more (legal) certainty than customary law. On the other hand, treaties are less easy to adapt.

A treaty can be defined as:
- an international agreement;
- between two or more subjects of international law;
- legally binding;
- subject to international law; and
- based on the consent of the parties.

Treaties can be classified according to their content as:
- creating law (*traités-lois*): this type of treaty creates new general rules of public law;
- contractual (*traités-contrats*): these international agreements establish mutual rights and obligations, and can be compared to private law agreements; and
- constitutional (*traités-constitution*): this type of agreement establishes international organisations and are often referred to as 'founding treaties'.

Depending on the number and the type of parties, a treaty may be classified as:

- bilateral (between two parties);
- multilateral (between three or more parties);
- mixed (between states and international organisations).

Treaties come in different forms and have different names. From a legal point of view, however, form and name are unimportant.

Example

A Memorandum of Understanding between two states is as much a treaty as the UN Charter or the Statute of the ICJ. On the other hand, the Charter of Economic Rights and Duties of States is not a treaty, but a non-binding resolution adopted by the UNGA.

23 Customary international law

Customary international law remains one of the most important sources of law in the absence of a central legislature and despite progressive codification of international law. Customary international law is created on the basis of:

- the practice of states; and
- the corresponding legal opinion that one should act in this way (*opinio juris*).

State practice

The practice of states:
- should be uniform and constant;
- does *not* need to exist for a long time, meaning that customary law can be formed almost immediately (*instant custom*);
- can be of a global, regional, or bilateral nature.

Opinio juris

The opinion that one is legally obliged to act in a certain way is called *opinio juris*. Identifying a particular opinion as a 'legal opinion' is more difficult than identifying an act relevant to the law. *Opinio juris* can be derived from:
- statements and actions by representatives of states;
- votes within international organisations;
- objections to the conduct of other states;
- national legislation.

A state will not be bound by a rule of customary international law if it consistently follows a different practice and/or view of the law. This creates the status of a *persistent objector*.

Example

An example of customary international law is the right of states to take action, under certain conditions, against unlawful acts of other states or the refusal of those states to compensate for damage resulting from such acts (see section 62).

24 Decisions of international organisations

The term *resolution* is a common name for decisions of international organisations. Decisions of international organisations can be either binding or non-binding.

Binding decisions

Most decisions of international organisations are recommendations and therefore *non-binding*. However, examples of binding decisions include:
- decisions of the UNSC under Articles 41 and 42 of the UN Charter; and
- decisions that have effect only within the organisation, such as budget decisions (e.g., Article 17 UN Charter).

Non-binding decisions

Non-binding decisions of international organisations are not legally irrelevant, however. They may serve as evidence of the existence of customary international law. Provisions in non-binding resolutions are also often qualified as *soft law*. This refers to a certain legal development where the rule has not yet crystallised into 'hard', positive law.

25 Other sources of law

The following sources of law are recognised in case law and literature:

- *General principles of law*: these can be both common principles of national law, such as 'good faith', and specific principles of international law, such as *pacta sunt servanda* (treaties must be respected).
- *Jurisprudence*: this category includes both national and international court decisions.
- *Doctrine*: the writings of important international law writers are losing ground as a source of law as more and more customary law is being officially codified. However, this source remains relevant for the development of international law.
- *Unilateral legal acts*: unilateral acts and declarations can, under certain circumstances, create obligations. However, the examples of international law are extremely limited.

Example

Following a complaint from Australia and New Zealand about French nuclear tests, the French president declared that he would stop nuclear testing. The ICJ considered this declaration to be legally binding.

- *Rules of mandatory law*: these are also called rules of *jus cogens*. They have an *erga omnes* character, that is they apply to all states.

Example

An example is the ban on (armed) force (see sections 64 and 65).

26 The relationship between international sources of law and legal rules

The following principles apply to a conflict between international sources of law and international rules of law:

- Rules of *jus cogens* (i.e., rules of mandatory law) take precedence; rules of international law that conflict with mandatory law are null and void.

- Conventions, customary laws, decisions of international organisations, unilateral legal acts, and general principles of law are regarded as equivalent sources. Conflicts between legal rules arising from these sources are therefore resolved through the application of adages:
  - □ new goes before old;
  - □ special goes before general;
  - □ old and special comes before new and general.
- Jurisprudence and doctrine are seen as complementary sources of law and are therefore hierarchically at the bottom.

Example

In 1970 two states concluded a special fishing treaty, unconditionally allowing each other's fishermen to fish in each other's territorial waters. In 1990 the same states ratified a general multilateral treaty on jurisdiction in the territorial sea, which stipulated that states could determine for themselves whether fishermen from other states were allowed to fish in the territorial sea. From 1990 the two states began to check whether fishing boats actually came from another state. A customary practice emerged that fishermen may be monitored. In this example, the older but more specific 1970 convention is not set aside by the newer but more general 1990 multilateral convention. However, the emergence of a more specific new customary law does alter rights under the 1970 convention. Fishermen from one state are still allowed to fish in the other state's territorial sea under the condition that their nationality may be checked.

Chapter V

Treaty law

27 Sources of treaty law

The general rules of treaty law can be found in:
- the 1969 Vienna Convention on the Law of Treaties (VCLT). This lays down the legal rules governing treaties between states;
- the Vienna Convention on the Law of Treaties between States and International Organizations or between International Organizations of 1986; and
- customary international law. There are two types of rules in customary international law:
  □ customary rules not codified in the aforementioned conventions; and
  □ customary rules that arose after the conclusion of the aforementioned conventions.

Special rules on the application and implementation of a treaty are to be found in the final provisions of the treaty itself.

28 The entry into force of treaties

The entry into force of treaties may require several
acts:

- *Signature*. The parties indicate their acceptance of
  the agreed text. This *concludes* a treaty. This means
  that the agreed text can no longer be changed. Signing
  may take place either:
  - □ subject to ratification, which means that:
    - the treaty does not enter into force; and
    - *no* treaty obligations are created, but under spe-
      cial circumstances there may be pre-contractual
      responsibility (Article 18 VCLT);
  - □ or not subject to ratification. The treaty will enter
    into force.
- *Ratification*. This is a formal act of the state and
  must be done explicitly. It will often be preceded by
  a process of parliamentary approval.
- *Accession*. Accession allows states that have not
  signed the treaty to become parties to it.

A treaty can enter into force at different times for different states:
- after it has been concluded, if no reservations or
  further rules have been laid down at the time of
  signing;
- at a specified time, as laid down in the treaty;
- after reaching the number of ratifications and/or
  accessions laid down in the treaty.

Example

The text of the VCLT was agreed on 23 May 1969. States had until 30 April 1970 to sign the convention. The convention entered into force on 29 January 1982. That is 30 days after the 35th state had ratified or acceded to the convention (Article 35 paragraph 1 VCLT). There are 116 states party to the treaty.

UK

The UK ratified on 25 June 1971. At that moment the VCLT entered into force for the UK.

29 Reservations

A reservation is an express declaration that the state does not consider itself bound by certain articles of a treaty. To determine exactly what obligations are incumbent on states under treaties, it is necessary to know:
- whether any reservations have been made. This can happen at:
  - signature;
  - ratification; or
  - accession;
- which reservations are permitted. It should be checked whether:
  - the treaty forbids reservations,

- □ the reservation is covered by reservations recognised by the VCLT; and
- □ the reservation is compatible with the purpose and object of the convention in question (Article 19 VCLT);
- which reservations have been accepted. If the treaty is silent, contracting parties may choose whether or not to accept reservations.

UK

The UK has made a reservation with respect to Article 66(b) of the VCLT, which concerns the jurisdiction of the ICJ.

30 Interpretation of treaties

The general rules of treaty interpretation are laid down in Article 31 VCLT:
- A treaty must be interpreted in good faith;
- in accordance with the ordinary meaning of the terms of the treaty;
- in their context; and
- in the light of the object and purpose of the treaty.

Article 31 contains no order of precedence with regard to the application of the grammatical, contextual, and teleological methods of interpretation. The historical method of interpretation is indicated in Article 32 VCLT as an additional means of interpretation.

31 The validity and effect of treaties

The validity and effect of a treaty may be challenged. Circumstances which become known after the treaty was concluded or which arise thereafter may render treaties:
- void or voidable; and
- terminated or suspended.

Table 1   Validity and effect of treaties

Legal consequence circumstance	Art. VCLT	Void	Voidable	Termination	Suspension
Infringement of national law or power of attorney	46–47	No	No	No	No
Mistake	48		Yes		
Deception	49		Yes		
Corruption	50		Yes		
Coercion	51	Yes			
Threat	52	Yes			
In breach of mandatory law	53–64	Yes			
Material breach	60			Yes*	Yes
Force majeure	61			Yes*	
Fundamental change of circumstances	62			No*	

*Exceptions to this general rule do exist

Apart from the circumstances mentioned above, a treaty can also be terminated if:
- there is agreement between the parties; or
- a timely notice of termination is given in accordance with the treaty provisions; or
- the term of the treaty has expired and there is no renewal.

32 State succession

The merging or break-up of states may affect the treaty obligations of those states. The following situations may arise:
- A state falls apart. In this case, it must be determined whether one of the new states can be considered as the successor of the old state. If the answer is:
  □ yes, then the successor state takes over the treaty obligations of the old state;

Example

The Soviet Union was dissolved by mutual agreement among its constituent republics. The Russian Federation has been accepted as the successor of the Soviet Union in international organisations.

  □ no, then the clean slate or tabula rasa principle is applied, that is the new states are not bound by any treaties of the old state, except for border treaties. In practice, new states tend to continue existing treaties.

Example

The Republic of South Sudan, became independent from Sudan in 2011. In that same year it applied to and became a member of the United Nations and the African Union.

The two constituent republics of Czechoslovakia decided by mutual agreement in 1992 to continue as new independent states: the Czech Republic and the Slovak Republic. Both states have reapplied for membership in international organisations. Financial and treaty obligations have been divided between them.

- Several states merge or the territory of a state is extended. Here the principle of mobile treaty borders applies, that is the obligations of the expanding state are transferred to the new territory.

Example

The German Democratic Republic was merged into the Federal Republic of Germany. In this case, only the scope and content of the takeover of the GDR's obligations by the FRG required determination. Membership of international organisations lapsed when the GDR ceased to exist.

- There is an internal change of power. Even if this change of power is accompanied by a change of the name of the state, treaty obligations remain.

33 National law and the entry into force of treaties

The VCLT does not prescribe how treaties are to be given effect in domestic law or what the constitutional procedures need to be for a state to adhere to an international treaty. Constitutional provision therefore differs between states. States, however, are not allowed to refer to domestic constitutional rules and procedures to justify a breach of treaty.

UK

In the UK, the executive (acting on behalf of the crown) is responsible for treaty-making and Parliament has no *formal* role. Even so, established practice means that many treaties are laid before Parliament for 21 days between signature and ratification. Previously known as the Ponsonby Rule, this practice was placed on a statutory footing by Part 2 of the Constitutional Reform and Governance Act 2010. Even despite this, the power to ratify the treaty remains with the executive and the role of the legislature is limited. The treaty takes binding force once it is ratified.

Chapter VI

Jurisdiction

34 Definition of jurisdiction

The jurisdiction of a state is exclusive, that is a state has sovereign power to the exclusion of other states. The jurisdiction of a state consists of three components:
- to make law (legislative power);
- to enforce the law (judicial power);
- to implement the law (executive power).

This exclusive jurisdiction is not unlimited or absolute. The extent and content of a state's jurisdiction is determined by:
- the territory of the state (territorial jurisdiction);
- nationality law and national criminal law (personal jurisdiction);
- international criminal law (see Chapter XVII);
- specific international legal regimes such as:
  □ diplomatic immunities (see section 47), which limit the state's jurisdiction; and

□ the UN Convention on the Law of the Sea (1982)
(UNCLOS), which determines the maritime zones
and can both extend and limit the jurisdiction of
the state.

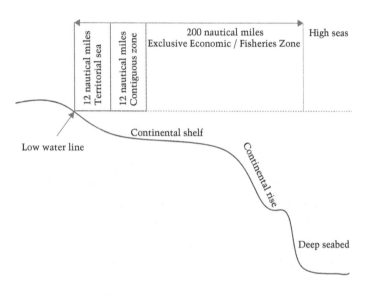

Not to scale

Figure 1 Cross-sectional diagram of maritime zones

35 Territorial jurisdiction

The fullest jurisdiction of a state extends over its territory, and is also called territorial jurisdiction. The territory includes:
• the land area;
• the inland waters; and
• the territorial sea.

State jurisdiction also extends to the subsoil (including raw materials) and airspace associated with these territories.

The extent of the maritime part of the territory of a state is determined by the so-called baselines. There are two types of baseline: the low-water line (Article 5 UNCLOS) and the straight baseline (Article 7 UNCLOS):

- A straight baseline may only be drawn between two land points if the total distance between these land points does not exceed 24 nautical miles.

UK

This is possible, for example, between the Hebrides Islands and the west coast of Scotland.

- Inland waters are on the land side of the straight baselines.
- The territorial sea is measured from the straight baseline and is a maximum of 12 nautical miles.

Ships in transit through the territorial sea have 'the right of innocent passage' (Articles 17–19 UNCLOS). This right is an exception to the exclusive jurisdiction of the coastal state.

36 Functional jurisdiction

A coastal state has functional jurisdiction to protect special rights and perform tasks. On the basis of

UNCLOS, states may claim functional jurisdiction over parts of the sea and/or seabed beyond the territorial sea.

- The *contiguous zone* (Article 33 UNCLOS) amounts to a maximum of 24 nautical miles from the straight baseline, or 12 nautical miles beyond the maximum extent of the territorial sea. The coastal state has specific powers in this zone to protect the territorial legal order, in particular in respect of the areas of imports, health, and migration.
- The *continental shelf* (Part VI UNCLOS) shall not exceed 350 nautical miles from the baseline. The coastal state has exclusive jurisdiction to explore and exploit the natural resources in the seabed of the continental shelf.
- The *Exclusive Economic Zone* (EEZ) (Part V UNCLOS) shall not exceed 200 nautical miles from the baseline. The right of the coastal state to explore and exploit natural resources in the EEZ extends to both the seabed and the water column. In this respect, the EEZ differs from the continental shelf regime. Within the EEZ, it is therefore also possible to exploit living natural resources. In contrast to the continental shelf regime, coastal states must specifically declare an EEZ (or exclusive fishing zone).

37 Areas outside national jurisdiction

No territorial jurisdiction can be claimed over the following areas:

- *The high seas*. This comprises all the area outside the internal waters, territorial sea, and EEZ of states (Article 86 UNCLOS). Here, all states have the right of navigation, overflight, exploitation, communication, and research, among others. Ships are subject to the jurisdiction of the flag state, unless:
  - □ the ship is arrested in hot pursuit of violations of rules in the contiguous zone or territorial sea of another state; or
  - □ there is good reason to enter the ship and carry out a further investigation on the spot (e.g. due to slave trade or piracy).
- *The ocean floor*. This has the status of 'common heritage of mankind'. In order to prevent states from claiming exploitation rights over the natural resources of the ocean floor, it comes under the 'jurisdiction' of the International Seabed Authority. The Authority is authorised to grant licences for exploitation of the seabed (Part X UNCLOS).
- *Space and the celestial bodies*. These, like the seabed, are classified as the 'common heritage of mankind'. The right to space and celestial bodies is enshrined in a large number of treaties, including the 1979 Treaty on the Moon and the older 1967 Treaty on the Use of Space. These treaties deny states the right to claim sovereignty over these areas.
- *Antarctica*. Due to the large amounts of natural resources that it contains, this is an area to which states have repeatedly laid claim in the past. However, these claims have been voluntarily

'frozen'. The 1959 Antarctic Treaty is the basis for the prohibition of exploitation of Antarctica's natural resources.

38 Demarcation of boundaries

Boundaries are drawn by mutual agreement. Special principles apply when delimiting the boundaries of border rivers, lakes, and maritime zones.

- The boundary in a river is determined by:
  - □ the so-called centreline, which at each point is equidistant from both banks; or
  - □ the channel, where both countries bordering the river can benefit from the transport possibilities offered by the river.
- The boundary between maritime zones can be defined by the so-called equidistance line. Each point on this line is equidistant from the adjacent or opposite coast. In many cases the technical application of this principle may lead to unfair results. Therefore, UNCLOS does not refer to equidistance as a delimitation principle. In several court cases the ICJ has pointed out the applicability of principles of reasonableness and fairness, which allow the interests of the countries concerned to be taken into account in the delimitation agreement.
- The demarcation of state boundaries is done by common agreement on the basis of general and specific international legal principles. Across continents

boundary claims have led to international disputes. Many of those disputes have been referred to the ICJ and arbitral tribunals. See for example:

- *Maritime Delimitation in the Caribbean Sea and the Pacific Ocean (Costa Rica v Nicaragua)* (2014),
- *Sovereignty over Pedra Branca/Pulau Batu Puteh, Middle Rocks and South Ledge (Malaysia/ Singapore)* (2003),
- *Territorial Dispute (Libyan Arab Jamahiriya/ Chad)* (1990).

UK

The delimitation of the continental shelf between the UK and France led to a legal dispute. When these states were unable to settle this dispute through negotiations which had begun in 1970, an arbitration agreement was signed by both parties in 1975. This led to the creation of an ad hoc court of arbitration which reached its decision in the *Delimitation of the Continental Shelf between the United Kingdom of Great Britain and Northern Ireland, and the French Republic (UK, France)* (1978) case. The purpose of this arbitration was to determine the seabed boundary between these two states in the English Channel. The significance of this case stems from the fact that it was only the second continental shelf boundary dispute to be settled by judicial means. In essence, the focus of the case was as to where lines of equidistance should be drawn and, crucially, how much weight should be given to several islands between these states in determining the point of equidistance. There were a number of lines of equidistance which needed to be determined and for each of these lines the respective islands were treated slightly differently.

39 Personal jurisdiction

The question of whether states can assert their jurisdiction over natural and legal persons outside their own territory is determined by:

- nationality (for private and criminal jurisdiction); and
- principles of criminal jurisdiction (see section 40).

Nationality is important in determining whether a person from state Y is also subject to the criminal law of state Y abroad, which family and personal law applies to them, and whether diplomatic protection can be granted by state Y (see section 52).

States decide for themselves how citizenship is granted. In most cases, this happens at birth. A child is then granted citizenship of:

- one or both parents (*jus sanguinis* principle); or
- the state of birth (*jus soli* principle).

After birth, citizenship can be acquired by naturalisation. International law requires that there be a real link between state and citizen.

Differences in nationality laws between states can under certain circumstances lead to statelessness or multiple nationality.

Example

Suppose that each parent comes from a state where the *jus sanguinis* principle applies (one parent from state A and one parent from state B) and the child is born on the territory of state C where the *jus soli* principle applies. In that case, the child will have a triple nationality. Conversely, a child born on the territory of state A or B to parents with state C nationality will not automatically receive a nationality at birth.

If multiple nationalities lead to conflicts between states concerning the exercise of diplomatic protection (see section 52), it should be established which nationality is the dominant one. Living and working conditions may be decisive in this regard.

The nationality of internationally operating legal persons can be determined on the basis of the actual seat (place of business) or the statutory seat (place of registration). The ICJ opted for the statutory seat in the *Barcelona Traction* case (1964).

40 Principles of criminal jurisdiction

A state can claim criminal jurisdiction on the basis of:
- the *subjective territoriality principle*, if the crime starts on its territory;
- the *objective territoriality principle*, if the crime is completed on its territory (effect doctrine);
- the *active nationality principle*, if a national is the perpetrator;
- the *passive nationality principle*, when a national is the victim – while the legitimacy of the application of this principle has long been disputed, with the increased focus on combating international crimes, it now seems to be increasingly accepted by states;
- the *principle of protection*, which empowers states to criminalise breaches of state security or public order. Terrorism as well as counterfeiting and conspiracy against the state may fall within the scope of the principle of protection; and
- the *principle of universality*, which creates the power for states to bring an internationally recognised crime under national criminal law. An example would be a crime against humanity. Such a crime need not have been committed in the prosecuting state, nor need the suspect be a citizen of the prosecuting state.

UK

Provided that the offence is one of a small number of serious offences, the UK may bring those accused of committing that offence in another country to justice in UK courts. This is known as 'universal jurisdiction'. In the UK, this applies only to the most serious international crimes such as, inter alia, war crimes, crimes against humanity, and torture. The UK government has published a note on the investigation and prosecution of crimes of universal jurisdiction.

Example

A national of state A is to detonate a bomb in state B on board an aeroplane from state C, which contains only tourists and crew members from state C. The bomb is to be detonated over state B with the intention of causing as much material damage as possible and destabilising the political order. Due to bad timing, the bomb is detonated earlier than planned over state D. All passengers and crew members are killed. State E considers this act to be terrorism and qualifies it as a conspiracy against State E.

In the case described above, each of the states – and each on the basis of a different principle – can claim jurisdiction over the alleged perpetrator and initiate proceedings. However, only the state in which the perpetrators are actually present has jurisdiction to arrest them and enforce the sentence imposed (see section 42).

41 National jurisdiction

States can in principle enforce their law on their own territory, in the territorial sea, and in the national airspace. This exclusive jurisdiction can be limited and extended on the basis of treaties and customary international law. States can also enforce their law on ships and aircraft on the basis of maritime law and aviation law agreements.

- Law of the sea: UNCLOS provides that ships have the nationality of the states in which they are registered (Article 91). There are exceptions to the exclusive right of the so-called flag state to enforce its law in respect of crimes such as piracy, drug and human trafficking, and environmental pollution.
- Aviation law: The Convention on Civil Aviation (1944) contains a similar provision for aircraft (Article 17). National law is therefore applicable on board aircraft.

The law of the national state may in certain cases lead to conflicts with another state that wishes to exercise its territorial jurisdiction.

42 Extradition

We saw earlier that jurisdiction has three components (see section 34). If a state wishes to enforce
its law (prosecute and/or enforce sentence), the person concerned must be in the territory of that state.
States may not enforce their law on the territory of
other states without the consent of the state where
the suspect is. Extradition is the process by which the
suspect is returned to the territory of the prosecuting state and is generally based on a treaty between
states.

Principles

The following extradition principles are commonly
accepted:

- The *dual criminality principle*: the act must be pun-
  ishable in both countries.
- The *principle of speciality*: trial may only be con-
  ducted on the basis of the offence for which the
  extradition was granted.
- The *ne bis in idem principle*: this excludes extradition where there has been a previous trial or impos-
  sibility of prosecution.
- The *aut dedere aut judicare principle* – on the basis
  of specific international obligations, states must
  either extradite or try: this principle is enshrined in
  various treaties on the protection of air traffic.

UK

The Extradition Act 2003 provides the legal basis for extradition to and from the UK and the European Union. For countries outside the EU, there is no statutory basis upon which the UK may request that individuals are extradited. Instead, the Home Office (a part of the executive) issues an extradition request under Royal Prerogative.

43 Domestic nationality law

International law does not prescribe how states determine and provide for citizenship: by birth, by descent, by naturalisation, or by succession of states (see section 39). Multiple nationalities can lead to competing claims concerning diplomatic protection (see section 52). Special rules apply to refugees and stateless persons.

UK

British nationality law provides for the conditions of British citizenship. Currently, the British Nationality Act 1981 determines who is a British citizen. British citizenship is acquired:

- By *lex soli*: by being born in the UK (or qualifying territory) provided that at least one parent is a British citizen or has settled in the UK (s.1.1); or at least one parent is a member of the armed forces (s.1.A).
- By *lex sanguinis*: by being born abroad provided that at least one parent holds British citizenship acquired *lex soli*. This limits the claiming of British citizenship 'by descent' to one generation.
- By naturalisation: the Home Secretary has the discretion to grant British citizenship. An application process and official requirements exist; however, the Home Secretary retains discretion over the granting of naturalisation.
- By registration: individuals born in the UK to parents neither of whom are British citizens are entitled to British citizenship after they have attained the age of 10 years provided that as regards each of the first 10 years of that person's life, the number of days on which they were absent from the UK in that year does not exceed 90 (s.4).
- By adoption: if a non-British minor is adopted by a British citizen habitually resident in the UK or in a designated territory, that minor acquires British citizenship (s.5).

Chapter VII

Immunities

44 Limitation of territorial jurisdiction

Immunities limit territorial jurisdiction. Persons or objects enjoying immunity cannot be subjected to the jurisdiction and/or law enforcement of the state in which they are located.

The main immunity beneficiaries are:

- states;
- representatives and affairs of states; and
- representatives and affairs of international organisations.

The main forms of immunity are:

- criminal immunity;
- private immunity; and
- immunity from taxation.

45 State immunity

States enjoy immunity in other countries. This is called state or sovereign immunity. With regard to state immunity, a distinction is made between:

- *acta jure imperii*: acts that can be considered to result from state law; and
- *acta jure gestionis*: acts of a private law nature, in other words the commercial acts of states.

In the latter case, the state takes part in legal transactions under private law in the same way as natural and other (legal) persons.

If a foreign state invokes state immunity before the courts, the latter will have to determine whether the state acted in its private law or in its state law capacity. This is determined by the national court on the basis of:

- the nature of the act; or
- the purpose of the actions.

The state enjoys absolute immunity for acts resulting from state law. Immunity cannot be claimed in respect of acts of private law.

Example

In the 2012 *Jurisdictional Immunities of the State (Germany v Italy: Greece intervening)* case, the ICJ confirmed the absolute nature of immunity for acts of state. The ICJ ordered Italy to refrain from implementing a judgment of the Italian court and to refrain from seizing German state property.

46 Derived immunities

Like the state, the highest representatives of the state also enjoy immunity. This immunity is considered to be derived from state immunity. The absolute nature of derived immunities is increasingly disputed. On the basis of standing jurisprudence and treaties, a number of rules can be established:

- Sitting heads of state, heads of government and foreign ministers enjoy absolute immunity under general international law in other states (ICJ ruling in *Arrest Warrant of 11 April 2000 (Democratic Republic of the Congo v Belgium)*).
- The ICC Statute provides that representatives of states shall not enjoy immunity in respect of offences defined in the Statute (Article 27(2) ICC Statute). The Statute deviates here from customary international law.
- Former representatives of states enjoy functional immunity. After the end of their term of office they can, under certain circumstances, be tried for internationally recognised crimes. These do not include acts done in the performance of duties related to the office (the *Pinochet case* – see section 106).
- Warships and other (non-commercial) vessels belonging to the state enjoy absolute immunity in

the ports, internal waters, and territorial sea of the coastal state.

47 Diplomatic immunities

Diplomatic missions are seen as necessary for the maintenance of relations between states. The law of diplomatic relations is one of the classic doctrines of international law.

The main rules on immunity of diplomatic representatives are found in both the 1961 Vienna Convention on Diplomatic Relations and in customary international law. Diplomatic immunities are granted by the receiving state after it has consented to the appointment of the ambassador of the sending state (Article 4 Convention on Diplomatic Relations).

Diplomatic immunities provide the following protection:

- Diplomats and their family members cannot be prosecuted at all. Private and administrative actions can only lead to limited lawsuits (purchase and sale of real estate and commercial activities by diplomats are excluded) (Articles 29 to 31 Convention on Diplomatic Relations).
- Technical and administrative staff enjoy the same criminal immunity. However, private and administrative immunity applies to this category of persons only when they are acting in the performance of their duties (Article 37(2) of the Convention on Diplomatic Relations).

- Diplomatic mail and correspondence shall not be opened or detained (Article 27 of the Convention on Diplomatic Relations).
- The embassy building and the Ambassador's residence may not be entered without permission (Article 22 in conjunction with Article 30 of the Convention on Diplomatic Relations).
- Diplomats are exempt from local taxation (Article 23 in conjunction with Article 34 of the Convention on Diplomatic Relations).

Diplomatic immunities entail a prohibition on enforcement. National law remains in full force, both on the embassy premises and for diplomatic staff.

Please note! An embassy is not foreign territory. Diplomatic personnel must abide by the laws of the host state.

Example

An embassy employee who shoots at a group of demonstrators from the embassy commits an offence under the law of the host state. However, diplomatic immunity prohibits their arrest and prosecution. The diplomatic post may not be searched for firearms and an abandoned embassy building is searched only in the presence of a foreign diplomat.

Waiving diplomatic immunity

A state can waive diplomatic immunity in one of two ways:

- *implicitly*: on the basis of conducting a defence in court, by which it can be assumed that immunity is not being invoked; or
- *explicitly*: on the basis of a formal (legal) act (*waiver of immunity*) by the state of the diplomat (Article 32 Convention on Diplomatic Relations).

If immunity is waived, a diplomat can be prosecuted under criminal law or sued in civil or administrative proceedings. Immunity must be waived separately for the judgment to be enforced.

Expulsion of diplomats

The receiving state can completely break off or suspend diplomatic relations, or expel one or more members of the embassy staff (declare them *persona non grata*) on two grounds (Article 9.1 Convention on Diplomatic Relations):

- The diplomat's activities and/or conduct are incompatible with their duties.
- As a measure of retribution for political reasons, by which the host state condemns the policies and/or actions of the sending state.

If diplomatic relations are broken or diplomatic personnel are declared *persona non grata*, the sending state should recall its diplomatic personnel within a 'reasonable period of time'. If this does not happen, the diplomats lose their diplomatic immunity (Article 9, paragraph 2 Convention on Diplomatic Relations). The receiving state must allow a reasonable period of time for the diplomats to leave the state.

The diplomatic mission

The diplomatic mission consists of:
- the Head of Mission – this may be (Article 14 Convention on Diplomatic Relations):
  - □ an ambassador or *nuncio*;
  - □ an envoy, minister or *internuntius*;
  - □ a *chargé d'affaires*;
- members of the diplomatic staff;
- members of the technical and service staff.

Example

The occupation of an embassy and the taking of the embassy staff as hostages is absolutely prohibited by international law. The ICJ has explicitly refused to accept any justification for such a breach of international law.

UK

In 2018 the UK announced the expulsion of 23 Russian diplomats following the poisoning of a former Russian military intelligence officer who was based in the UK. These diplomats were given a week to leave the UK. In response to this, Russia ejected 23 British diplomats and ordered the closure of the British Consulate in St Petersburg. In situations like this, the expelled diplomats should be given a reasonable amount of time to leave the state.

Chapter VIII

State responsibility

48 State responsibility

The main rules in the area of state responsibility are laid down in the draft articles on the Responsibility of States for Internationally Wrongful Acts (State Responsibility). The draft contains two types of rule:

- Codified rules of customary law: these rules create obligations for states because they are part of customary international law.
- New rules: these have been formulated and advanced by the International Law Commission in a progressive development of the law. They are not binding, as they are not customary law or treaty rules.

The articles concentrate on the general conditions for, and consequences of, state responsibility. The traditional rules of state responsibility (i.e., rules on the treatment of foreign (legal) persons) are not explicitly included in the draft.

49 International wrongful acts

State responsibility arises out of an international wrongful act (Article 1 State Responsibility). An international wrongful act can be defined as an act or omission of a state that:
- is attributable to the state; and
- constitutes a violation of an international obligation of that state (Article 2 State Responsibility).

Attribution

An act can be attributed (imputed) to a state if it is an act or omission of:
- organs with legislative, executive, judicial, or other powers – a state *cannot* invoke the autonomy or independence of state organs as a justification;

Example

A court judgment, or a decision of lower authorities or a public body, may lead to the responsibility of a state.

- (a group of) persons recognised or influenced by the state – these need not be officials or agents of the state;

Example

The action of a group of students, as in the 1979 Iran hostage crisis at the USA's embassy in Iran, may lead to state responsibility.

• liberation movements if a movement takes over governmental power or creates a new state;

Example

South Africa can be held accountable for past international wrongful actions of the ANC.

• citizens of the state in some circumstances, for example when the state fails to prevent reasonably foreseeable damage to the property of other states or foreign nationals (*due diligence*). This means that reasonably foreseeable damage to the property of other states or foreign nationals must be prevented. If this obligation is breached, state responsibility arises.

Example

If a mass demonstration against a particular state is announced, states must take measures to protect that state's embassy as unrest is foreseeable.

Violation of international law

A violation of international law occurs when a state's actions do not comply with what is required by an applicable obligation. The origin of the obligation is irrelevant, as is the nature of the infringement. An international wrongful act may continue in time insofar as the factual and/or legal consequences of an unlawful act have not been undone.

50 Circumstances precluding wrongfulness

The unlawfulness of a culpable breach of an obligation may be excused under certain circumstances. A state may invoke six circumstances as defences:

- *Consent*: if the 'injured' state has consented to a specific conduct, it can never lead to responsibility.
- *Self-defence*: the unlawfulness was the result of an in itself lawful exercise of the right of self-defence.
- *Countermeasures*: the violation constitutes a measure against a previous violation of an obligation of the 'injured' state. The right of states to take 'countermeasures' is not unconditionally accepted in the articles on State Responsibility. In this area, there is a legal development that goes too far for some states and not far enough for others.
- *Force majeure*: this may be invoked if the state is unable to perform the obligation due to an unforeseeable and uncontrollable event. It may be that a strict responsibility rests on the state.

- *Distress*: the violation must be aimed at protecting the acting person's own life (or the life of others).
- *Necessity*: this exceptional circumstance may only be invoked if an act is necessary for the protection of an essential interest against a serious and imminent danger. In addition, the 'necessary' act must not infringe an essential interest of another state.

These defences cannot be used to preclude wrongfulness, that is as a defence to non-conformity with an obligation arising under *jus cogens* (see section 21).

51 Cessation and compliance

The injured state may demand that:
- the obligation breached is materially fulfilled;
- the unlawful act or omission is terminated;
- guarantees are provided that no repetition will occur;
- the material and immaterial damage is completely repaired.

Recovery can take place in various ways:
- The person entitled is actually and/or legally restored to the original state (*restitutio in integrum*).
- Compensatory damages are paid (compensation). This is only possible for an assessable and determinable damage including determined loss of profit in so far as the damage has not been repaired by *restitutio in integrum*.

• Satisfaction takes place. To the extent that the damage cannot be repaired by *restitutio in integrum* or compensatory damages, another means of satisfaction may be required. This can be both an acknowledgement of the violation of the international obligation and the offering of a formal apology or expression of regret.

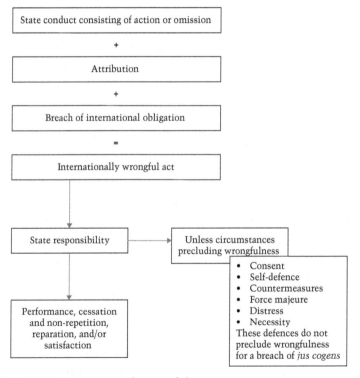

State conduct consisting of action or omission

+

Attribution

+

Breach of international obligation

=

Internationally wrongful act

State responsibility	→	Unless circumstances precluding wrongfulness

Performance, cessation and non-repetition, reparation, and/or satisfaction

- Consent
- Self-defence
- Countermeasures
- Force majeure
- Distress
- Necessity

These defences do not preclude wrongfulness for a breach of *jus cogens*

Figure 2 International wrongful act

52 Diplomatic protection

Diplomatic protection should not be confused with diplomatic immunity! Diplomatic protection can only be exercised by states:

- on behalf of their own nationals or legal persons whose rights have been violated abroad – the state does this on its own account and has discretionary power, that is nationals cannot demand or renounce diplomatic protection; and
- if all local remedies have been exhausted (the *local remedies rule*), unless it is clear that the use of local remedies is not possible or not effective. This may occur if the person concerned has been deported and is not allowed to return, or if national courts reject claims by foreigners in a standard procedure.

Diplomatic protection is often provided if citizens are treated unlawfully. There are two views on how foreign nationals should be treated:

- *national treatment*, that is the treatment of foreign nationals is equal to the treatment of nationals; and
- *international minimum standard*, that is the treatment of foreign nationals should be in accordance with internationally agreed standards.

The recognition of international human rights has rendered the controversy between the two views as regards the treatment of citizens of other states obsolete.

Diplomatic protection is also available where there has been nationalisation of property in violation of international standards, but only under the following conditions:

- the public good must be served;
- discrimination is prohibited;
- real damages must be paid immediately in common currency (prompt, adequate, and effective); and
- all local remedies need to be exhausted (the local remedies rule), unless it is clear that local remedies cannot be exhausted or are ineffective.

Chapter IX

Settlement of disputes

53 General and special rules

States are obliged to settle their disputes in a peaceful manner. This general customary law obligation is elaborated in:

- international treaties, such as the UN Charter (Article 2.3 in conjunction with Article 33);
- UNGA resolutions, such as:
  - □ The Declaration on Principles of International Law Concerning Friendly Relations and Cooperation (UNGA Resolution 2625); and
  - □ The Manila Declaration on the Peaceful Settlement of International Disputes (UNGA Resolution 37/10);
- regional conventions, such as the American Treaty on Pacific Settlement (Pact of Bogotá) (1948).

Freedom of choice and consent are the guiding principles in international dispute resolution, with mandatory dispute resolution being an exception.

International dispute resolution is characterised by the following interrelated developments:

- *Fragmentation*: each international organisation and each treaty regime have their own dispute resolution procedure.
- *Institutionalisation*: non-legal methods of dispute resolution are enshrined in treaties.
- *Specialisation*: new procedures are being developed and new tribunals set up to deal with specific circumstances.

54 Diplomatic methods

Resolution of issues by diplomatic methods differs in a number of ways from other means of dispute resolution.

- Diplomatic methods are more flexible and less procedural than arbitration and litigation.
- These 'alternative' dispute resolution methods have been formalised and institutionalised in a number of conventions and organisations.
- The result is not binding.

The following diplomatic methods can be distinguished:

- *Negotiation*: this takes place between the contesting parties and requires no third-party involvement. As a result, the course of the negotiation process is determined solely by the negotiating parties.
- *Good offices*: the third party is passive during the negotiation process and serves as a communication channel.

- *Mediation*: the third party is active and contributes to the resolution of the dispute.
- *Investigation*: the third party establishes 'facts' and reports on them.
- *Conciliation*: the third party formulates a proposal that should lead to the settlement of the dispute.

Many arbitration and court cases are preceded by one or more of these processes.

55 International arbitration

Arbitration has the following characteristics:
- It may be ad hoc or institutionalised. The influence on the procedure and the freedom of choice regarding arbitrators decreases the more arbitration is institutionalised.
- The arbitral award is binding on the parties.
- Depending on the parties involved, arbitrations can be qualified as:
  - □ public law arbitration (between states): the PCA was established as early as 1899. This institution provides a secretariat, a list of possible arbitrators, and premises to hold discussions;
  - □ private or commercial arbitration (between private parties);
  - □ mixed arbitration (between a state or an IGO and a private party): disputes about agreements between states and companies are often subject to international law. Investment disputes by states are

governed by a treaty that provides for ISCID. The arbitration between Sudan and the Sudan People's Liberation Army before the PCA also falls into this category.

In order to be able to settle a multitude of legal claims, so-called *mixed claims tribunals* are often set up. In principle, these tribunals can settle both public and private law and mixed claims cases. Examples are the Iran–United States Claims Tribunal set up in 1981 and the Eritrea–Ethiopia Claims Commission set up in 2000.

UK

The UK is or has been involved in arbitration cases such as:

- The *Anglo-French Continental Shelf case* (1978). This case concerned the delineation of the continental shelf boundaries of the UK and France.
- *Ireland v United Kingdom (OSPAR Arbitration)* (2003). This case concerned the commissioning of a mixed oxide nuclear fuel reprocessing plant.
- *MOX Plant Case (Ireland v United Kingdom)* (2008). This case once again concerned a mixed oxide nuclear fuel reprocessing plant, albeit the

focus here was the discharge of waste from this plant into the Irish Sea.

- *Guaracachi America, Inc. (USA) & Rurelec plc (United Kingdom) v Plurinational State of Bolivia* (2014). Investment was the focus of this arbitration.
- *Chagos Marine Protected Area Arbitration (Mauritius v United Kingdom)* (2015). This arbitration focused on the administration of the Chagos Archipelago, a group of islands in the Indian Ocean.

56 The International Court of Justice

The ICJ is considered the prototype of institutionalised dispute resolution. The ICJ has a number of specific features.

- The ICJ is the primary judicial body of the UN. UN Member States are parties to the Statute of the ICJ. States are not obliged to accept the jurisdiction of the ICJ (Article 92 UN Charter).
- The ICJ has a permanent character. The judicial panel consists of 15 judges. Parties not represented on the panel may appoint a so-called ad hoc judge. The judges represent the main legal systems and are elected for a minimum of nine years by the UNGA in cooperation with the UNSC.

- The ICJ has a dual role:
  - □ judging, that is passing judgments in interstate disputes; and
  - □ giving advice in legal matters at the request of a UN body (advisory opinion).
- Its procedures are laid down in the Statute and the Rules of Court of the ICJ.
- Decisions in interstate disputes are binding (Article 94 UN Charter).

The jurisdiction of the ICJ

The ICJ has no mandatory jurisdiction. Acceptance of the jurisdiction of the ICJ can be by means of:
- *a compromise*: this is a bilateral agreement whereby the parties to the agreement jointly recognise the jurisdiction of the ICJ for that particular case and refer any dispute to the ICJ;
- *a compromise clause*: this is a dispute settlement clause in a bilateral or multilateral agreement that allows a state to unilaterally bring a dispute before the ICJ;
- *making a declaration:* unilaterally accepting the jurisdiction of the ICJ over any state that does the same. However, reservations can be attached to this declaration, which does not achieve the intended result (a system of compulsory international jurisdiction), since temporal and material limitations can be placed on the jurisdiction of the ICJ. As the

optional clause system is based on reciprocity, the system is thus eroded;
- *a factual act*: an act from which it may be inferred that jurisdiction has been assumed (*forum prorogatum*).

UK

While the UK had previously accepted the compulsory jurisdiction of the ICJ, a 2017 Declaration contains the latest recognition of this compulsory jurisdiction. The UK has been involved in the following cases:

- *Corfu Channel (United Kingdom of Great Britain and Northern Ireland v Albania)* (1946–1948). Three judgments between 1946 and 1948 assessed Albanian liability for the explosion of naval mines which damaged British warships passing through the Corfu Channel in 1946.
- *Fisheries (United Kingdom v Norway)* (1951). The UK challenged the method used by Norway in drawing baselines (see section 35) as contrary to international law.
- *Anglo-Iranian Oil Co. (United Kingdom v Iran)* (1951). Iran nationalised its oil industry, which undermined a previous agreement between, and in turn created a dispute between, Iran and the Anglo-Iranian Oil Company. The UK took up the company's case.

- *Ambatielos (Greece v United Kingdom)* (1952). The Greek government took up the claim of one of its nationals, who claimed to have suffered damage due to the UK's failure to carry out the terms of a contract for the purchase of ships.
- *Minquiers and Ecrehos (France/United Kingdom)* (1953). France and the UK agreed to ask the ICJ to determine which state had the most convincing proof to title of a group of islets situated between Jersey and France.
- *Monetary Gold Removed from Rome in 1943 (Italy v France, United Kingdom of Great Britain and Northern Ireland, and United States of America)* (1954). This case centred on a dispute as to how gold recovered during the Second World War should be distributed.
- *Antarctica (United Kingdom v Argentina) and Antarctica (United Kingdom v Chile)* (1956). The UK brought a dispute against Argentina and Chile concerning sovereignty over certain lands and islands in the Antarctic.
- *Aerial Incident of 27 July 1955 (United Kingdom v Bulgaria)* (1959). The UK sought to bring a claim for the loss of British nationals killed during the destruction of an aircraft by Bulgarian anti-aircraft defences.
- *Northern Cameroons (Cameroon v United Kingdom)* (1963). In the context of decolonisation,

the Republic of Cameroon claimed that the UK had violated a trusteeship agreement.

- *Fisheries Jurisdiction (United Kingdom v Iceland)* (1974). The UK and the Federal Republic of Germany challenged Iceland's proposed extension to the limits of its exclusive fisheries jurisdiction.
- *Questions of Interpretation and Application of the 1971 Montreal Convention arising from the Aerial Incident at Lockerbie (Libyan Arab Jamahiriya v United Kingdom).* This long-running dispute stemmed from Libyan objection to the charging and indictment of Libyan nationals relating to the Lockerbie bombing. Specifically, the dispute before the ICJ sought to clarify the interpretation and application of the 1971 Montreal Convention.
- *Legality of Use of Force (Serbia and Montenegro v United Kingdom)* (2004). The Federal Republic of Yugoslavia instituted proceedings against several countries (including the UK) for alleged violations of their obligation not to use force against another state.
- *Obligations concerning Negotiations relating to Cessation of the Nuclear Arms Race and to Nuclear Disarmament (Marshall Islands v United Kingdom)* (2016). The Marshall Islands – where many nuclear weapons had

been tested – claimed that the UK (and other states) had failed to honour a non-proliferation treaty.

The contentious procedure

As soon as a case is brought, the preparations for handling the main case begin.

- Preliminary objections may be raised. These objections may relate to:
  - □ the competence of the ICJ. This ICJ competence is absent if there is no specific legal basis or if a reservation made applies;
  - □ the admissibility of the claimant state. A state is not admissible if, for example, there is no demonstrable (legal) interest, local remedies have not been exhausted, or diplomatic protection may not be exercised.
- If the jurisdiction of the ICJ is contested, the proceedings in the main action will be stayed, that is the ICJ must first rule on its jurisdiction before proceeding to the main action.
- Provisional measures may be requested. These can be taken if the rights of the state deserve immediate protection.
- Intervention requests may be made by a third-party state. Third-party states must demonstrate that they are affected in a legal sense by a possible ruling.

The decision

The ICJ delivers a judgment by a majority of votes. The judgment is reasoned. The opinions of judges with dissenting opinions (those belonging to the minority) and judges with separate opinions (those belonging to the majority for reasons other than those mentioned in the judgment) are attached to the judgment.

There is no possibility of appeal against the judgment. A ruling may be brought to the attention of the UNSC or lead to a request for interpretation and/or review.

The advisory procedure

At the request of the UNGA, the UNSC, or other authorised UN bodies and organisations, the ICJ can issue an opinion on specific legal questions or issues, such as the use of nuclear weapons, the construction of a wall in occupied Palestinian territory, and the forced closure of a PLO office in New York. The rulings in an advisory procedure are not binding.

57 The International Tribunal for the Law of the Sea

The International Tribunal for the Law of the Sea (ITLOS) was established in 1996 within the framework of UNCLOS. ITLOS is based in Hamburg and has 21 judges. Its procedure can be compared to that of the ICJ, that is the Tribunal can deliver judgments and opinions.

The Tribunal's jurisdiction relates primarily to the interpretation and application of UNCLOS. In addition, some six conventions contain dispute settlement clauses that refer to ITLOS. A special Chamber has been established for disputes relating to decisions of the International Seabed Authority. The Tribunal may decide to hear cases in chambers.

UK

In 2021 ITLOS confirmed that Mauritius has sovereignty over the Chagos Islands and urged the UK to end its unlawful occupation of the territory.

58 The panel procedures of the World Trade Organization

The current WTO dispute settlement system has its origins in the panel procedure that existed under the GATT (General Agreement on Tariffs and Trade 1947). It is elaborated in the Dispute Settlement Understanding (DSU). This annex to the WTO Treaty provides for three bodies:

- The *Dispute Settlement Body* (DSB). The DSB is composed of representatives of all WTO Member States. This body has the power to:
  □ establish a panel of experts;

☐ accept or reject panel reports and Appellate Body reports;

☐ monitor the implementation of rulings and recommendations; and

☐ authorise the taking of countermeasures.

- *Panels*. These panels assess the dispute in the first instance. Panels are set up for each dispute. Their conclusion must enable the DSB to make a recommendation or a decision in the dispute. Panel reports do not constitute precedent. They do, however, form part of the WTO body of rules.
- The *Appellate Body*. This body reviews the panel report on appeal at the request of one of the parties. On appeal, only points of law and questions of legal interpretation may be raised.

The procedure

A number of stages can be distinguished in the WTO panel procedure:

- The *investigation phase*. After the panel has been established by mutual agreement, it examines the complaint.
- The *interim review stage*. At this stage, the panel submits its description of the dispute and the interim conclusions to the parties for comments.
- The *final report*. The final report is sent to the DSB and the parties. The parties may appeal the panel's conclusions.

- The *appeal*. The Appellate Body assesses the case on appeal.
- The *implementation phase*. The DSB adopts the Panel or Appellate Body report. The losing party indicates how it will implement the report. If a dispute arises over implementation, the DSB may grant permission to impose trade sanctions. This is called 'suspension of concessions or other obligations under the covered agreements' and is subject to arbitration.

UK

Three complaints have been brought against the UK:

- in 1997 by the USA regarding the customs classification of certain computer equipment;
- in 2004 by the USA regarding the provision of subsidies to the aircraft industry;
- in 2006 the USA brought a second complaint regarding the provision of subsidies to the aircraft industry.

---

59 The Inspection Panel of the World Bank

In 1993 the World Bank created a procedure to allow affected individuals and NGOs to file a complaint against a particular project. The complaint must allege violations of World Bank policies and procedures. The Inspection Panel consists of three panel members. A panel proceeding consists of three stages:

- *The investigation at first instance.* On this basis, the Panel recommends to the Board of Directors whether or not to undertake a further investigation. The Board has a discretionary power to accept or reject the recommendation. In the first case, the complaint is referred back to the Panel.
- *The investigation.* The Panel has far-reaching powers to collect information.
- *The decision-making process.* Based on the Panel's final report, the Board makes a final decision. All reports, recommendations, and decisions are public.

Complaints are eligible if:
- the Complainant can establish a link with the project area;
- the Bank fails to comply with its policy and thereby causes harm;
- the Bank's management has been informed and its response is unsatisfactory;
- all formalities are met.

Chapter X

The enforcement of international law

60 Characteristics of the enforcement of international law

The enforcement of international law is character-ised by:

- *the absence of a central authority*: states must enforce their rights themselves when they are violated;
- *the legitimacy of one's own action*: states can take non-military coercive measures individually and collectively. Collective measures are often taken within the framework of international organisations;
- *the existence of a general prohibition of the use of (armed) force*. Exceptions are:
  - □ self-defence (Article 51 UN Charter); and
  - □ with the consent of the UNSC (Article 42 UN Charter).

61 Retorsion

Retorsion is retaliatory action taken by a state. There are several things to note about such an approach:
- Retorsion measures are lawful.
- Taking retorsion action is an unfriendly act.
- Retorsion measures can target both unlawful and unfriendly conduct of other states.
- Most coercive measures fall into the category of retorsion.

UK

After the then Prime Minister David Cameron met the Dalai Lama in 2012, China froze diplomatic relations with the UK. This ended after 14 months with an agreement that the prime minister would visit China.

Example

Recalling or expelling ambassadors, breaking off negotiations, boycotting meetings, and imposing stricter visa requirements are examples of unfriendly but legitimate measures.

62 Reprisals

Reprisals (also called countermeasures) are a violation of one or more obligations towards another state. The unlawfulness of reprisals is removed if a number of conditions are met (Articles 49–54 State Responsibility):

- The countermeasure must be a reaction to a preceding unlawful act.
- The countermeasure must be proportionate. In determining proportionality, the seriousness of the wrongful act and the rights infringed must be taken into account.
- The measure must be lifted at the cessation of the preceding unlawful act. Thus, the measure may not be of a punitive nature.
- Measures must not contravene obligations imposed by mandatory international law, humanitarian law, and/or diplomatic relations.

Example

The freezing of a foreign state's assets and the non-execution of (reciprocal) treaty obligations are examples of countermeasures.

63 Collective measures

Constitutive conventions of international organisations may provide for a power to take collective measures (also known as sanctions). A violation of the substantive or institutional law of that organisation by a Member State leads to the deprivation of rights or to the imposition of sanctions. The UN Charter provides for various measures against violations of UN law:

- Member States that 'persistently violate the principles of the Charter' can be expelled from the UN (Article 6 UN Charter).
- Member States that are in arrears with their contributions for at least two years can be deprived of their right to vote (Article 19 UN Charter).
- States and other international entities that pose a threat to international peace and security may be subject to military and non-military measures under Chapter 7 of the UN Charter ('Action with regard to threats to peace, breach of peace and acts of aggression').

Economic measures by the UNSC

The UNSC can require UN Member States to take coercive measures to implement or reinforce binding UNSC decisions. These measures may lead, among other things, to 'the complete or partial severance of economic relations and of rail, sea, air, postal, telegraphic and radio communications, and other links, and the severance of diplomatic relations' (Article 42 UN Charter).

The UNSC can also issue sanctions against non-state organisations, such as the Taliban, Al-Qaeda, and ISIS, as well as individuals. UN Member States will also have to implement these decisions. Such measures may include freezing bank accounts, issuing travel bans, and an arms embargo.

Table 2 Examples of economic measures against states by the UNSC

Measure	Against	On the basis of	Year
Travel and financial measures	South Sudan	UNSC res. 2428	2018
Travel ban/asset freeze (individuals)	North Korea	UNSC res. 2356	2017
Export ban on luxury goods	North Korea	UNSC res. 2094	2013
No-fly zone	Libya	UNSC res. 1973	2011
Import ban on diamonds	Liberia	UNSC res. 1343	2001
Diplomatic boycott	Sudan	UNSC res. 1070	1996
Oil embargo	Haiti	UNSC res. 841	1993
Arms embargo	Yugoslavia	UNSC res. 713	1991
Trade and arms embargo	Iraq	UNSC res. 661	1990

UK

The UK currently has a number of sanctions regimes in force. The government is empowered to undertake these via legislation. Sanctions regimes may be instigated under, inter alia, the Sanctions and Anti-Money Laundering Act 2018 and under other UK legislation such as the Export Control Order 2008 and the Anti-Terrorism, Crime and Security Act 2001.

Chapter XI

Peace and security

The lawfulness of the use of armed force in war and conflict situations must be judged on two different legal bases. First, it must be established whether (military) force may be used as an exception to the general prohibition on the use of force (*jus ad bellum*). Second, it must be established whether the manner in which this is done is in accordance with the rules of international humanitarian law (*jus in bello*).

64 The prohibition of (armed) force

Article 2(4) of the UN Charter prohibits 'the threat or use of force against the territorial integrity or political independence of a State or in any other manner inconsistent with the purposes of the UN'. This prohibition is seen as a codification of binding customary international law. The prohibition of (armed) force was further elaborated in the Declaration on Friendly Relations (1970) and the Declaration on the Definition of Aggression (1974).

65 Exceptions to the prohibition on (armed) force

The UN Charter allows only two formal exceptions to the general prohibition of (armed) force:

- (Collective) Self-defence (Article 51 UN Charter): a state may defend itself (possibly assisted by other states) against an 'armed attack' by another state. This is subject to a number of conditions:
  □ An armed attack must have taken place. Anticipatory self-defence action is prohibited. There is controversy surrounding what constitutes an armed attack.
  □ The (armed) force used in self-defence must be proportionate to the attack and aimed at driving the attacker back.
  □ Self-defence actions must be reported to the UNSC.
  □ Self-defence actions must cease once the UNSC has taken the 'measures necessary to ensure international peace and security'. There is controversy over what 'measures' should be considered 'necessary'.
- A mandate from the UNSC (*enforcement action*) (Article 42 UN Charter): the UNSC can grant states the authority to use military force, after the UNSC has determined that:
  □ there is a threat to or a breach of international peace and security or an act of aggression (Article 39 UN Charter); and
  □ this situation continues.

The UNSC has a far-reaching mandate to determine when use of (armed) force is warranted. The veto system (see section 75) prevents Article 42 from being used frequently. The question whether the UNSC has granted a mandate for the use of (armed) force, and on what grounds, can be answered in different ways on the basis of the text of the relevant resolution.

UK

The question whether the participation of British troops and army units in Iraq in 2003 was lawful could not be ruled upon by the Chilcot Inquiry. Even so, the report of that inquiry found that the legal basis for war was 'far from satisfactory'.

Contested exceptions to the prohibition on (armed) force

In addition to the exceptions described above, there are two less widely recognised exceptions that are regularly referred to by states to justify the use of military force:

- Freeing or protecting nationals abroad. The deployment of military forces abroad to protect nationals is not uncommon. In civil wars and hostage-taking situations, states often opt for a military solution. Such deployment of military forces is not a legitimate exercise of the right of self-defence and violates the territorial integrity of the other state.

- Humanitarian intervention is seen by some as a justified use of military resources abroad for the benefit of (part of) the population there. The risk of abuse and selective use of humanitarian intervention is high. The deployment of military means with an appeal to the humanitarian situation is therefore viewed very critically by most authors.

Table 3   Legal basis for the use of force

Qualification	Violence against	On the basis of	Year
Responsibility to protect	Libya	UNSC res. 2009	2011
UNSC mandate	Rwanda	UNSC res. 929	1994
UNSC mandate	Somalia	UNSC res. 794	1992
UNSC mandate	Iraq	UNSC res. 678	1990
Self-defence	Argentina	Art. 51 UN Charter	1982

66 UN peace operations

The 'UN peacekeeping operation' differs from coercive military action under Article 42 of the UN Charter in the following respects:
- There is no legal basis for it in the UN Charter. UN peacekeeping operations have developed on the basis of UN practice.
- The stationing of a peacekeeping force is subject to the consent of the state. States are not obliged to accept peacekeeping forces on their territory.

- The use of force mandate is limited, that is the armament is geared to self-defence.
- Peace forces are neutral, that is they are not a party to the conflict.
- The supreme command is formally in the hands of the UN.

Types of peace operations

The aforementioned differences between peacekeeping and peace enforcement are diminishing. The (enforcement) mandate of peacekeeping forces is expanding and the type of conflict in which peacekeeping forces are deployed is changing. The following types of peace operations can be distinguished:
- *Classic* peacekeeping operations:
  □ take place in an interstate conflict;
  □ act as a buffer and/or supervise a truce between two states; and
  □ have a mainly military component.
- *Humanitarian* peacekeeping operations are deployed in internal conflicts and aim at:
  □ the restoration of public order and authority within a state – besides a military task, these peace operations often have police tasks as well; and
  □ facilitating humanitarian aid – military and humanitarian tasks go hand in hand.
- *Supporting* peacekeeping operations aimed at the reconstruction of society within a state. Military

tasks are replaced by judicial, humanitarian, and political tasks.

Peacekeeping operations can be used preventively. Their success is highly dependent on the will of the warring parties and the agreement of the warring parties to the peacekeeping mission is a necessary condition for employment of a peacekeeping force. Participation in or financing of UN peacekeeping missions is not compulsory.

67 International humanitarian law

The answers to the questions of which persons and buildings may be regarded as military targets, which means of war may be used, and how prisoners of war and civilians should be treated during war are mainly to be found in the Geneva Conventions:

- the First Geneva Convention for the Amelioration of the Condition of the Wounded and Sick in Armed Forces in the Field (1864);
- the Second Geneva Convention for the Amelioration of the Condition of Wounded, Sick and Shipwrecked Members of Armed Forces at Sea (1906);
- the Third Geneva Convention relative to the Treatment of Prisoners of War (1929);
- the Fourth Geneva Convention relative to the Protection of Civilian Persons in Time of War (1949).

The four conventions were merged in 1949 and later expanded to include:

- the First Additional Protocol on the Protection of Victims of International Armed Conflict (1977);
- the Second Additional Protocol on the Protection of Victims of Non-International Armed Conflicts (1977); and
- the Third Additional Protocol on the Adoption of a Supplementary Distinctive Emblem (2005). In addition to the 'Red Cross' and the 'Red Crescent', the 'Red Diamond' is now also used as an identifying mark.

68 The International Committee of the Red Cross

In relation to international humanitarian law, the ICRC is the most important non-state organisation to which tasks are assigned by treaty. Several articles in the Geneva Conventions mention the ICRC by name (see, for example, Article 10 of the Fourth Geneva Convention). The importance of the ICRC is also reflected in its status as *observer* to the UNGA (see section 83). The ICRC also has a special position in international criminal law. However, there are still major differences of opinion regarding the international legal personality of the ICRC (see section 20).

Chapter XII

The law of international organisations

69 Development of international organisations

The establishment of international organisations can be explained by the need of states to work together towards common goals. The first international organisations therefore had a functional character. After the First World War, they increasingly took on a political character. The development of international organisations after 1945 is characterised in the following ways:

- *Globalisation*: organisations such as the UN have grown from 51 members in 1945 to 193 in 2011. Other global organisations have similar membership numbers. Their powers are more specialised and limited (see Chapter XIV).
- *Regionalisation*: states cooperate in organisations that are limited to continents, such as the AU, or regions, such as the Association of South-East Asian Nations (ASEAN) (see Chapter XV).

- *Socialisation*: states establish organisations and bodies that deal with social problems, such as the environment (United Nations Environmental Program) and human rights (UN Human Rights Council).

The developments outlined above have led to complexity in organisational structures, decision-making procedures, and competences. These developments deserve a separate treatment of the law of international organisations (also called international institutional law). Institutional law, like the substantive law of international organisations, is mainly to be found in the founding treaty of the organisation concerned.

70 Classification of international organisations

International organisations can be classified according to different criteria:
- *Membership*. On this basis, a distinction can be made between open or universal and closed or non-universal organisations. Closed organisations can only be joined by countries that have specific and objective characteristics, such as geographical location or the presence of certain raw materials. Many open or universal organisations belong to the UN family (see Chapter XIII).
- *Objective*. Organisations can be qualified on the basis of their objective as general (political) organisations or specific (functional) organisations.

- *Powers.* Supranational organisations are distinguished from intergovernmental organisations on the basis of their competences. In supranational organisations, binding decisions can be taken by majority vote. This is not possible in purely intergovernmental organisations. Most organisations are intergovernmental.

Table 4   Classification of international organisations

Organisation	Membership	Objective	Powers
UN	Open	General	International
WTO	Open	Specific	International
EU	Closed	General	Supranational
OPEC	Closed	Specific	International

71 Membership of international organisations

Organisations have different forms of participation in their work:
- *Ordinary or full membership* is granted to states and possibly other international organisations.
- *Associate membership* is an opportunity for components of a state or prospective Member States to participate in the organisation's decision-making.
- *Observer status* may be obtained by entities that are not state or intergovernmental in nature or by states that do not wish to become members.

The manner and conditions under which these various forms of participation are granted or withdrawn are determined by the founding treaty or by secondary legislation.

Loss of membership

Membership of international organisations may be lost for the following reasons:

- The state or organisation is dissolved. It is not common for organisations to dissolve themselves. The dissolution of the Western European Union (WEU) in 2011 and the Warsaw Pact (1991) are unique exceptions. Merging into a new organisation is more common.
- States withdraw from organisations. The institutional law of some organisations provides for this. If no provision is made for the power of states to withdraw from membership, the question arises whether withdrawal is a lawful act.
- The organisation deprives the state of membership.

72 Structure of international organisations

The structure of an international organisation is reflected in the founding treaty. Most organisations have different bodies with their own powers and tasks. The most common bodies are as follows:

- A *plenary body*. This represents all members and is charged with general (policy) matters and setting the budget, among other things. Many plenary bodies are not permanent but meet only once or

twice a year. Examples are the UNGA, the WTO
Ministerial Conference and the Council of the
North Atlantic Treaty Organization (NATO).

- *Non-plenary bodies.* These are composed of a limited number of members and are entrusted with specific tasks. Depending on the nature of the task, such
a body may be permanent or non-permanent: for
example, the UNSC.
- A *secretariat.* This is permanent in nature and is
responsible for the preparation and execution of the
day-to-day business of the organisation. Secretariat
staff members are expected to be independent, (geo-
graphically) representative, effective, honest, and
competent.
- A *judicial body* charged with settling disputes
between members of the organisation or between
the organisation and its employees.

73 Powers of international organisations

International organisations derive their powers on the
basis of the principle of attribution directly or indirectly
from the consent of the participating states, as follows:

- Explicitly granted powers are found in the founding
treaty.
- Non-explicitly granted powers must be derived from
the (explicitly formulated) tasks and objectives of
the organisation via the doctrine of implied powers.
- The powers of the organisation as such must be distinguished from the powers of individual bodies.

- In addition to rights, international organisations also have duties and can therefore be held liable for international wrongful acts.

74 Decision-making procedures of international organisations

Decisions of international organisations can be distinguished as:
- *binding or non-binding decisions*: most decisions of international organisations are not binding on Member States;
- *decisions having internal or external legal effects*: decisions with exclusively internal legal effects include, for example, appointment decisions and budget decisions;
- *procedural or non-procedural decisions*: decisions on the setting of meeting topics and agendas are procedural in nature. Decisions taken on a particular conflict are non-procedural.

The founding treaty often specifies the effect of decisions and how they are made.

75 Rules of procedure of international organisations

Decisions are made on the following bases:
- *Consensus.* In this case, *no vote* is taken. The chairperson formulates the perceived consensus as a decision if no protest is made.

- *Voting.* When voting is used, it must be determined:
  - □ what weight a vote has:
    - In principle, each member of an organisation has only one vote (*one state, one vote*) without special qualification.
    - With weighted voting, the 'weight' of the vote is considered. This can be determined on the basis of financial contribution (International Monetary Fund – IMF), production and/or consumption quotas (Organization of the Petroleum Exporting Countries – OPEC) or population size (EU).
    - So-called vetoes have a negative weight. This vote is intended to block decisions.
  - □ which voting ratio is necessary for decision-making. The voting ratio has three modalities:
    - *unanimity.* Unanimity is deemed to exist if none of the members vote against;
    - *simple majority*, that is half plus one of the votes;
    - *qualified majority*, for example two-thirds or three-quarters of the votes.

The *rules of procedure* may specify which 'votes' count in decision-making:
- The votes of *all members* (including those not present). If more than half of the members are not present at the vote, no majority decision can be taken.
- The votes of the *members present*. The vote of an absent member does not count in the decision-making. Absence is insufficient to prevent majority decision-making.

- The votes cast (*members present and voting*). Not voting does not influence the decision-making.

76 Budgetary affairs of international organisations

The determination of an organisation's income and expenditure is a binding decision. Income can be obtained by:
- contributions determined on the basis of equality or ability to pay;
- donations from private or public funds;
- own resources (taxes, patents, investments).

Expenditure can be divided into:
- administrative expenses (e.g., salaries and buildings);
- operational or project expenditure (e.g., peacekeeping, humanitarian aid, and education).

77 Immunities and privileges of international organisations

There is hardly any customary international law in this area of law. Privileges and immunities of international organisations can be characterised as functional. General and special rules can be found in treaties:
- *specific treaties*, such as the Convention on Privileges and Immunities of the United Nations (1946) (CPIUN);

- *founding treaties* (e.g., Article 105 UN Charter);
- so-called *headquarters agreements* concluded between the organisation and the 'host state'.

Four different types of immunity beneficiaries can be distinguished:
- The international organisation itself:
  - □ Property, possessions, archives, and diplomatic missions are inviolable.
  - □ Bank balances, assets, and incomes are exempt from taxation.
  - □ Communication must not be impeded (Articles 2 and 3 CPIUN).
- Officials of the organisation, who possess immunities and privileges necessary for the performance of their duties. These include:
  - □ decisions and actions taken in the performance of their duties, and
  - □ criminal and private immunity (in exceptional cases).
- Representatives of Member States, members of national delegations, and observers, who enjoy privileges and immunities comparable to diplomatic immunities (Article 4 CPIUN).
- Experts of the organisation, who are not considered officers of the organisation but do enjoy immunity from prosecution. Their mail and luggage also enjoy immunity.

Example

In two different advisory procedures, the ICJ was able to specify the status of 'experts' and the extent of their immunity. In the Advisory Opinion on Article VI, Section 22 of the Convention on the Privileges and Immunities of the United Nations, the ICJ determined that the term 'expert' should be interpreted broadly and that a 'mission' continues as long as the specific task is not completed. In the Advisory Opinion on a Dispute concerning Immunity from Criminal Prosecution of a Special Rapporteur of the UN Commission on Human Rights, the ICJ noted that a UN Rapporteur also enjoys immunity in their own state if they make statements by virtue of their office. It is up to the UN Secretary-General to determine whether certain statements were made in the exercise of their duties.

78 Responsibility of international organisations

With the increased activities of international organisations, the regulation of their responsibility for wrongful acts is also becoming increasingly important. In 2011 the UNGA took note of the Draft on Responsibility of International Organizations by the International Law Commission (UNGA Res. 66/100I). The draft broadly follows the rules on the Articles on State Responsibility.

Chapter XIII

The United Nations

79 Foundation and development

The UN Charter was signed on 26 June 1945 and entered into force on 24 October 1945. Its headquarters are located in New York. Other important bodies are located in The Hague, Vienna, Geneva, and Nairobi.

Since its creation, the UN has undergone a number of important developments:

- The number of Member States has increased from 51 to 193. The accession of new states has changed the voting ratio in the UN.

UK

The UK is a founding member of the United Nations and became a member on 24 October 1945.

- The UN Family has grown (see Figure 3).

- In addition to developing policy, the UN has been given a large number of executive tasks (e.g., in the field of peacekeeping, promotion and monitoring of human rights, and humanitarian aid).

80 Objectives and principles

Article 1 of the UN Charter states the following objectives:
- the maintenance of international peace and security;
- developing friendly relations between states;
- developing international cooperation to solve socio-economic, cultural, and humanitarian problems;
- to act as a centre for harmonising the actions of states in pursuit of these objectives – this should be regarded as a means rather than an objective in its own right.

Article 2 of the UN Charter formulates the principles that apply in the pursuit of these objectives. The most important are:
- sovereign equality of the Member States;
- abstinence from (armed) force;
- peaceful settlement of disputes;
- respect for the territorial integrity of the Member States.

81 UN organs

The following bodies can be distinguished within the UN organisation:
- The six *main bodies* (Article 7 UN Charter).

Table 5   Main UN bodies

Organ	Composition	Meetings	Location	UN Charter
UNGA	All members UN	1 x per year	New York City	9–22
UNSC	15 members (5 permanent)	Permanent	New York City	23–32
Economic and Social Council	54 UN members	1 x per year	New York City	61–72
Trustee Council	The 5 permanent members of the UNSC (China, France, the Russian Federation, the UK and the USA)	As required	New York City	86–91
International Court of Justice	15 judges	Permanent	The Hague	92–96
Secretariat	Independent staff members	Permanent	New York City	97–101

- *Auxiliary bodies* (Article 7.2 UN Charter). These are often subdivided into:
  - □ Subsidiary bodies established by the UNGA or the UNSC when necessary for the exercise of the functions of the UN. Examples of subsidiary bodies are the Human Rights Council, peace missions, and the Counter-Terrorism Committee.

☐ Programmes and funds instituted by the UNGA. They differ from other subsidiary bodies in that they have their own budget and secretariat, and non-Member States can also participate in these bodies. Examples are the UN Environment Programme (UNEP), the UN International Children's Emergency Fund (UNICEF) and the UN Development Programme (UNDP).

☐ Committees instituted by the UN Economic and Social Council (ECOSOC) (Article 68 UN Charter). These can be divided into:
- regional commissions, such as the Economic Commission for Europe;
- functional commissions, such as the Commissions on Narcotics, Population, or Statistics;
- permanent committees, such as the Committee on Non-Governmental Organizations.

In addition to the aforementioned UN bodies, the UN family also includes specialised agencies (Article 57 of the UN Charter). These are established on the basis of a treaty. A specialised agency maintains a formal contractual relationship with ECOSOC (Article 63 UN Charter). Such specialised agencies include the WHO, the International Labour Organization (ILO), the International Civil Aviation Organization (ICAO), and the International Maritime Organization (IMO) (see also Chapter XIV).

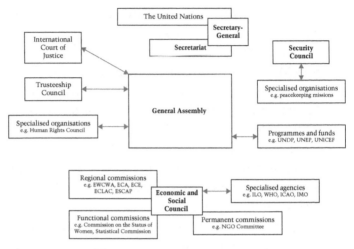

Figure 3 Basic UN organogram

UK

The UK is a permanent member of the UNSC. Additionally, the UK currently serves as a member of ECOSOC (until 31 December 2023) and the Human Rights Council (until 31 December 2023).

82 Relationships between the different UN bodies

The bodies of the UN have different formal relationships with each other on the basis of the UN Charter. There is a general reporting obligation for all bodies to the UNGA (Article 15 UN Charter). Depending on the decision to be taken, different bodies may be involved in the decision-making process:

- Admission of new members: recommendation by the UNSC and decision by UNGA (Article 4 UN Charter).
- Exclusion of members: recommendation by the UNSC and decision by UNGA (Articles 5 and 6 UN Charter).
- Peace and security: the UNGA and the Secretary-General can make recommendations to the UNSC (Article 10 in conjunction with Articles 11 and 99 UN Charter).
- ECOSOC may make recommendations to the UNGA on matters within its competence (Article 62 UN Charter).
- The Secretary-General reports annually to the UNGA on the work of the UN (Article 98 UN Charter).

Example

The constitutional relationship between the UNGA and the UNSC has been the subject of a dispute concerning the admission of a state to the UN (1947) and whether the UNGA could authorise expenditures for a UN peacekeeping force (1961).

83 Powers and functions of UN agencies

The powers and functions of the UN are formulated in the UN Charter. Different functions, powers, and duties can be defined for each body.

- The UNGA (Articles 10–17 UN Charter):
  □ can deal with all matters within the scope of the UN Charter;
  □ must take into account the competence of the UNSC in the area of international peace and security;
  □ does not, apart from decisions addressed to internal organisations, take binding decisions. The resolutions adopted by the UNGA are therefore formally only recommendations.
- The UNSC (Articles 23–54 UN Charter) is responsible for the maintenance of international peace and security (Article 24 UN Charter). To this end, it may determine that there is a breach or threat to international peace and security and take military and non-military measures to maintain international peace and security (Article 39 in conjunction with Articles 41 and 42 UN Charter).
- The Economic and Social Council (Articles 61–74 UN Charter):
  □ can produce or commission studies and reports on economic, socio-cultural, and educational issues;
  □ can make recommendations in the area of human rights; and
  □ can draft treaties.

- The Trusteeship Council (Articles 86–91 UN Charter) is (co)responsible for governing so-called trust territories for which the UN has responsibility. As these no longer exist, the Trusteeship Council is de facto non-functioning.
- The ICJ (Articles 92–96 UN Charter):
  □ can settle disputes with the consent of states; and
  □ provides legal advice at the request of, inter alia, the UNGA and the UNSC.
- The Secretariat (Articles 97–101 UN Charter):
  □ supports the main organs;
  □ has a Secretary-General with its own power to refer matters of international peace and security to the UNSC.

84 The voting procedures in the UN

In the UN each member has one vote. The voting ratio is determined by the nature of the decision.

Table 6   Voting in the UN

Decisions	General Assembly	Security Council	Economic and Social Council	Trusteeship Council
Ordinary and procedural matters	Majority of members present		Majority of members present	Majority of members present
Important matters	2/3 members present			

Table 6   (cont.)

Decisions	General Assembly	Security Council	Economic and Social Council	Trusteeship Council
Procedural matters		9 out of 15 members		
Non-procedural matters		9 out of 15 members, including permanent members		

85 Immunities and privileges of the UN

The immunities and privileges of the UN are set out in various documents:
- The UN Charter (Article 105).
- The Convention on the Privileges and Immunities of the United Nations (1946). This treaty contains provisions regarding:
  □ property, funds, and assets (Article II);
  □ the freedom of communication (Article III);
  □ the immunity of state representatives, staff, and experts (Articles IV–VI); and
  □ travel documents (Article VII).
- The Headquarters Agreement between the United Nations and the United States of America (1946). The Headquarters Agreement provides in particular:
  □ the territory in which the UN is established and the authority of the UN over that territory (Articles II and III);

- □ communications and travel to and from the UN premises (Article IV);
- □ the protection and provision of public services to the UN (Articles VI and VII).
- The Convention on the Privileges and Immunities of the Specialized Agencies of the United Nations (1947) mirrors the provisions of the 1946 Convention, except that annexes contain specific provisions for individual specialised agencies.

Example

In 1988 the ICJ ruled that the USA was under an obligation to accept international arbitration concerning a dispute with the UN.

86 The responsibility of the UN

Closely linked to the privileges and immunities of the UN is the question of the accountability of this organisation. More so than other international organisations, the UN is involved in humanitarian, reconstruction, and military interventions. The question of who is responsible for the damage caused by UN activities cannot remain unanswered.

Example

In 2007 a number of Bosnian women held the UN liable for 'the fall of Srebrenica and the consequences thereof'. In 2008 the Court of The Hague deemed itself 'incompetent to take cognisance of the claim against the United Nations' with an appeal to the 'absolute immunity of the United Nations'. In April 2009 a Memorandum of Grievances was filed, specifically challenging the view that the District Court would have no jurisdiction to hear claims against the UN. In 2010 the Court of Appeal in The Hague upheld the ruling of the District Court, and in 2012 the Supreme Court upheld the judgments of the District and Appeal Courts.

The United Nations Administrative Tribunal (UNAT) is an independent UN body that decides on employment disputes between the UN and UN staff.

87 The UN and the development of international law

The UN plays an increasingly important role in the development of international law. It does this by:
• organising conferences for the establishment of conventions (e.g., UNCLOS, ICC);

- codifying and developing areas of law through the UN's International Law Commission;
- contributing to the formation of state practice through the adoption of resolutions;
- enforcing international law through UNSC resolutions; and
- adopting declarations and resolutions which stipulate general principles of law.

Chapter XIV

Other global international organisations

88 Comparison with the United Nations

In addition to the UN, there are about twenty other global organisations. These may differ from the UN in the following areas:

- *Functional specialisation*: for example, there are organisations for postal traffic, nuclear energy, food and agriculture, and telecommunications.
- *Powers*: None of the global organisations has the supranational powers of the UN in the fields of peace, security, and humanitarian action.
- *Decisions and decision-making*: declarations and opinions are not binding. It is therefore not possible for these organisations to respond effectively and decisively to threats to peace and security.
- *Composition*: The above also results in these organisations having fewer bodies and committees. The secretariats of these organisations reflect the functionality of the organisation.

89 The International Labour Organization

The ILO was founded in 1919, has 187 members and is based in Geneva. This organisation has a number of unique features:

- The delegations of the Member States have a tri-partite structure. Each delegation consists of two government representatives, one employers' repre-sentative, and one employees' representative.
- Each member of the delegation has one vote.
- Conventions may be adopted in addition to recom-mendations. The latter must be ratified in accord-ance with the rules of treaty law. Signature is not a requirement (see section 28).

Since 2012 the ILO has had its own supervision system based on:

- a reporting obligation of the Member States;
- the lodging of a complaint on the basis of trade union freedom or bargaining freedom;
- the filing of a specific complaint by an organisation of workers or employers; or
- the lodging of a complaint by one Member State against another Member State.

Currently, 35 complaints have been lodged by 29 Member States, which have led to 13 Commissions of Inquiry.

UK

The UK was a founding member of the ILO. As such, it became a member in 1919 and has ratified 87 conventions including all eight of the fundamental conventions. It has not been the subject of a complaint.

90 The World Health Organization

The WHO was established within the framework of the UN in 1948, has 193 members, and is based in Geneva. Its features are as follows:

- It has a limited mandate. In the field of international health care, the organisation mainly provides assistance and promotes international cooperation (Article 2 WHO Treaty).
- It has an Assembly, an Executive Board, and a Secretariat, headed by the Director-General.
- The Assembly can adopt treaties (which enter into force according to the rules of treaty law) and make recommendations.

The role of the WHO in combating the COVID-19 virus in 2020 gives a good overview of its tasks. The WHO can inform, advise, and coordinate but cannot take actions itself.

UK

The UK is a founding member of the WHO, which was founded in 1948.

Example

The rights and powers of the WHO were the subject of a dispute between Egypt and the WHO, which led to an Advisory Opinion by the ICJ (1980).

91 The International Civil Aviation Organization

The ICAO was established in 1947 on the basis of the Convention on International Civil Aviation (1944, as amended in 2006), has 193 members, and is based in Montreal, Canada. The powers of the ICAO are subordinate to the sovereignty of the Member States over their airspace (see also section 41). Air traffic between states is regulated by bilateral treaties.

The objectives of the ICAO are (Article 44 ICAO Convention):

- developing the principles and techniques of international aviation; and
- promoting policy and development on international air transport.

Its main bodies are the Assembly, the Council, the Aviation Commission, and the Secretariat. The Council consists of three groups of states:

- states of chief importance in air transport;
- states making the largest contribution to facilitating international civil air navigation; and
- other states to ensure that all major geographic areas of the world are represented.

Disputes regarding the interpretation or implementation of the ICAO Convention may be decided in the first instance by the Council (Article 84 ICAO Convention). However, the organisation has no independent dispute resolution instrument.

Example

The Civil Aviation Convention was the subject of a court case before the ICJ, brought by India against Pakistan in 1972 (*Appeal Relating to the Jurisdiction of the ICAO Council*).

Article 26 of the ICAO Convention obliges Member States to initiate an investigation into aircraft accidents.

UK

The UK has been a member of the ICAO since the organisation was founded in 1947.

92 The International Maritime Organization

The IMO was founded in 1958 on the basis of the Convention on the International Maritime Organization (1948). It has 174 members and is based in London.

The IMO has been responsible for the drafting of some thirty specific conventions designed to enhance maritime safety and protect the maritime environment. These include conventions on port facilities.

The main objectives of the IMO are set out in Article 1 of the IMO Convention. These are:

- facilitating cooperation on technical matters and promoting the adoption of standards for safe shipping; and
- promoting freedom of navigation.

In particular, the organisation has an advisory and consultative role (Article 2 of the IMO Convention). This includes:

- making recommendations;
- designing treaties and other regulatory instruments;
- establishing a consultation mechanism;
- facilitating technical cooperation.

In addition to a General Assembly and a Council, the IMO has a number of special committees in the fields of:

- maritime safety;
- legal affairs;

- protection of the maritime environment; and
- technical cooperation.

The IMO Council has three membership categories:
- 10 states with the largest interest in providing international shipping services;
- 10 states with the largest interest in international seaborne trade;
- 20 states not elected under the two above categories but which have special interests in maritime transport or navigation and whose election to the Council will ensure the representation of all major geographic areas of the world.

UK

The UK has been a member of the IMO since 1958.

Chapter XV

Regional intergovernmental organisations

93 The Organization of American States

The Organization of American States (OAS) was established in 1948 and has its seat in Washington DC. All countries in the Americas except Cuba are members. The Charter of the Organization of American States has been amended four times (1967, 1985, 1992, and 1993).

Its main objectives are:
- the promotion of peace, security, and democracy (Article 1(a) and (b));
- the settlement of disputes (Article 1(c) and (e)); and
- the promotion of economic, social and cultural development (Article 1(f)).

Its main bodies are:
- the General Assembly;
- the Permanent Council;
- the Secretariat; and
- the Inter-American Committee of Human Rights.

The OAS does not have its own regional court of justice to settle inter-state disputes. The Inter-American Court of Human Rights is not an OAS body, but it does monitor the observance of human rights by OAS Member States.

94 The European Union

The EU was established in 1993 by the Maastricht Treaty. The EU consists of 27 Member States and has its headquarters in Brussels. The EU Treaty has been amended three times (1999, 2003, and 2009). The legal basis for the EU was the Treaty of Paris (1952), establishing the European Coal and Steel Community, and the Treaty of Rome (1958), establishing the European Economic Community and the European Atomic Energy Community. The legal and institutional structure of the EU is the most complicated and advanced of all regional intergovernmental organisations. Because of its far-reaching powers, the EU is also referred to as a supranational organisation.

Its main objectives are (Article B Maastricht Treaty):
- to establish an economic and monetary union;
- to develop cooperation in the field of justice and home affairs;
- to develop a common peace and security policy;
- to enhance the rights of EU citizens.

Its main organs are:
- the European Council (representing Member States);

- the European Parliament (representing the citizens of the Member States);
- the European Commission (the EU government);
- the Court of Justice (competent in cases between Member States, between Member States and citizens, between Member States/citizens and the EU, and between EU bodies).

95 The African Union

The AU was established in 2002 and has its seat in Addis Ababa, Ethiopia. The AU consists of 53 Member States. The AU replaces the Organization of African Unity (OAU), established in 1963 and dissolved in 2002. The Constitutive Act concluded in Lomé (Togo) has only 33 articles. A number of important issues have been left open to be elaborated in additional protocols.

Its main objectives are to:
- promote unity and solidarity, and political and socio-economic integration (Article 3(a) and (b));
- promote living standards, democracy, and human rights (Article 1(g), (h) and (k));
- promote the status and role of (the Member States of) Africa in the world (Article 1(f)).

Its main organs are:
- the Assembly (representing Member States);
- the Executive Council (Ministers of Foreign Affairs);
- the Pan-African Parliament;
- the Court of Justice;

- the Financial Institutions (the African Central Bank, the African Monetary Fund, and the African Investment Bank);
- the Commission (AU Secretariat).

96 The Association of Southeast Asian Nations

ASEAN was established in 1967 on the basis of the Bangkok Declaration, a non-binding document. ASEAN has its seat in Jakarta, Indonesia, and has 10 Member States. In 2007 the Member States adopted the ASEAN Charter. This 55-article treaty gives ASEAN an international legal basis. A number of important issues have been left open to be elaborated in additional protocols.

Its main objectives are:
- the promotion of peace and security (Article 1(1));
- the promotion of socio-economic and political cooperation (Article 1(2));
- the creation of an internal market (Article 1(5));
- the strengthening of democracy and the promotion of human rights (Article 1(7)).

Its main organs are:
- the Summit (Heads of State or Government) (Article 7);
- the Coordinating Council (Ministers of Foreign Affairs) (Article 8);
- Community Councils (Article 9);
- the Sector Councils (Article 10);
- the Secretariat (Article 11);

- the Committee of Permanent Representatives (Article 12);
- the Human Rights Body (Article 14).

ASEAN does not have a court of justice and, as with the AU, many treaty provisions need to be further elaborated.

97 Other regional intergovernmental organisations

In addition to the organisations mentioned above, there are numerous other organisations which have cooperation within a specific region as their objective. A large number of these regional organisations have an economic objective, such as the North American Free Trade Association (NAFTA), the Economic Community of West African States (ECOWAS), and the Benelux (Belgium, the Netherlands, and Luxembourg) Union (see section 118). Regional organisations such as the Arab League and the Council of Europe (CoE) have a more political character. Examples of more functional regional organisations are the organisations for the management of cross-border rivers, such as the Rhine Commission or the Zambesi River Authority. Several regional organisations also exist in the field of fisheries, such as the North Atlantic Fisheries Commission.

UK

The UK is a member of the following regional organisations:

- The CoE (est. 1949) is a typical international organisation with 47 European Member States. The Council has a 318-member Parliamentary Assembly, a Committee of Ministers, and a Secretary-General. Under its auspices more than two hundred treaties have been concluded, the most well-known being the European Convention on Human Rights and Fundamental Freedoms (1953), which has its own independent Court: The European Court of Human Rights (see section 103).
- The European Space Agency (est. 1975) has 22 Member States (including Canada). It initiates civil space projects including research and the development of satellite systems.

Chapter XVI

International human rights

98 Recognition and development

International human rights and the international criminal responsibility of individuals were more clearly recognised only after the Second World War. Human rights have been further developed on the basis of the *non-binding* Universal Declaration of Human Rights (UDHR). The current human rights treaty catalogue consists of a large number of specific and general treaties and regional and national case law.

The duties of individuals are reflected in particular in the Statute of the International Criminal Court and the Hague and Geneva Conventions on the humanitarian law of war. The trials at Nuremberg (for political leaders and military personnel from Nazi Germany) and Tokyo (for military personnel from Japan) after the Second World War were key to the development of individual criminal responsibility. This has been further developed with the establishment of the Yugoslavia

Tribunal, the Rwanda Tribunal, and the International Criminal Court.

99 Categories of human rights

Human rights can be classified as follows:
- *Civil and political rights*, the classical freedom rights, which are characterised by:
  - □ their focus on the protection of the citizen from the state – the political freedom of the citizen and state abstinence are central;
  - □ their immediate obligations – the obligation of the state to produce results; and
  - □ the connection of these rights with liberal thinking.

Examples

Examples of civil and political rights are the right to freedom of expression, the right to freedom of religion, and the right to association.

- *Economic, social, and cultural rights*, whose characteristics are:
  - □ their focus on the socio-economic well-being of citizens and their cultural identity and freedom;
  - □ their non-immediate obligations – the state's obligation is to take steps to actively promote these rights. Except for the standards of the minimum

core obligation, guaranteeing a certain result is not immediately required; and
□ their relationship with the socio-economic ideology of socialist states and developing countries.

Example

Examples of economic, social, and cultural rights are the right to work, the right to education, the right to food, and the right to clothing.

* *Collective rights*, which are characterised by:
  □ a transcending of the individual interest;
  □ the recognition of the existence of minorities and indigenous peoples; and
  □ the abstract and political nature of these rights.

Example

Examples of collective rights are the right to self-determination and the right to a habitable environment.

For historical and political reasons, civil and political rights, on the one hand, and economic, social, and cultural rights, on the other, have often been laid down in separate treaties. In specific human rights treaties, such as those on women's rights or children's rights, both types of rights can be found together.

100 International human rights instruments

Human rights can be found in various international binding and non-binding documents:

- The UDHR (1948) contains a compilation of political, social, economic, and cultural rights. The declaration itself is not binding. However, most of the rights enshrined in it are binding through treaties and/or customary law.
- The UN international human rights instruments are:
  □ International Covenant on Civil and Political Rights (ICCPR 1966);
  □ International Covenant on Economic, Social and Cultural Rights (ICESCR 1966);
  □ Convention on the Rights of the Child (CRC 1989);
  □ International Convention on the Elimination of All Forms of Racial Discrimination (ICERD 1965);
  □ Convention on the Elimination of All Forms of Discrimination Against Women (CEDAW 1979); and
  □ Convention against Torture and Other Cruel, Inhuman or Degrading Treatment or Punishment (UNCAT 1984).
- Special treaties, including:
  □ The Convention Relating to the Status of Refugees (The Refugee Convention 1951);

□ the UN Educational, Scientific and Cultural Organization (UNESCO) Convention against Discrimination in Education 1960; and
□ ILO Conventions for the protection of workers.

101 Implementation and enforcement mechanisms in international human rights treaties

Each of the above-mentioned treaties has provisions and procedures to guarantee the rights set out in them. Four enforcement mechanisms can be distinguished:

• *The individual's right of complaint.* On the basis of this, the individual citizen has direct access, without state intervention, to an international court or a committee which can examine the complaint and issue a ruling or a recommendation.
• *The state's right of complaint.* This gives states the power to file a complaint against other states on the basis of alleged violations of certain human rights. This possibility is hardly ever used by states.
• *The reporting obligation.* This requires states to report on the implementation and development of legal provisions for the protection of human rights. The reports submitted by states may be assessed on the basis of information from other sources (e.g., NGOs).
• *The right of investigation.* Human Rights Commissions are empowered to investigate on their own behalf alleged human rights violations or the situation and/or developments with regard to a recognised right or in a particular state.

Table 7 Implementation and enforcement mechanisms in international human rights treaties

Convention	Entry into force	Individual Right to complain	State Complaint Law	Reporting	Right of investigation	UK's ratification status
Elimination of All Forms of Racial Discrimination	21 December 1965	Optional	Yes	Yes		Signature 1966; ratification/accession 1969
Civil and Political Rights	23 March 1976	Optional	Optional	Yes	Yes	Signature 1986; ratification/accession 1976
Economic, Social, and Cultural Rights	3 January 1976	Optional	Optional	Yes	Optional	Signature 1968; ratification/accession 1976
Elimination of All Forms of Discrimination against Women	3 September 1981	Optional	Optional	Yes	Optional	Signature 1981; ratification/accession 1986
Against Torture and Other Cruel, Inhuman, or Degrading Treatment or Punishment	26 June 1987	Optional	Yes	Yes	Yes*	Signature 1985; ratification/accession 1988

Protection of Migrant Workers and their Families	18 December 1990	Not yet entered into force	Optional	Yes	No	Signature N/A; ratification N/A
Rights of Persons with Disabilities	03 May 2008	Optional	No	Yes	Optional	Signature 2007; ratification/accession 2009
Protection of All Persons from Enforced Disappearance	23 December 2010	Optional	Optional	Yes	Optional	Signature N/A; ratification N/A
Rights of the Child	02 September 1990	Optional	Optional	Yes	Optional	Signature 1990; ratification 1991

*Exceptions to this general rule do exist

Optional = the state must have explicitly accepted the competence of the relevant committee in the treaty or in an optional protocol

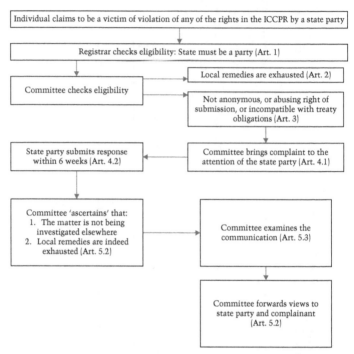

Figure 4 Example individual complaint procedure (ICCPR)

Note: Individual communications may only be brought under the ICCPR if the Respondent State is a Party to the Optional Protocol to the International Covenant on Civil and Political Rights (1996).

102 Monitoring mechanisms

Monitoring mechanisms, in addition to enforcement and implementation mechanisms, play an important role in respecting human rights. Important monitoring mechanisms are:

- The *UN Human Rights Council*. The Council was established in 2006 by the UNGA and will replace the UN Commission on Human Rights. In addition to monitoring compliance, the Council will work on the development and promotion of human rights.
- The *UN High Commissioner for Human Rights*. This official mainly has a signalling role. In addition, other human rights instruments are supported.
- The *OSCE* provides for the possibility of sending fact-finding missions to countries where human rights violations are alleged.
- The *OSCE High Commissioner on National Minorities* (HCNM). This High Commissioner has their own authority to take initiatives in the area of minority protection in the OSCE Member States.

103 Regional human rights instruments

In addition to the international human rights instruments, many regions and regional organisations have their own human rights treaties, declarations, and implementation and monitoring mechanisms.

UK

The UK is party to:

- The European Convention on Human Rights and Fundamental Freedoms and as such has accepted the jurisdiction of the European Court of Human Rights.
- The European Social Charter. As the UK has not ratified the revised charter, it has not accepted the authority of the independent Committee of Social Rights.

Table 8 Regional human rights instruments

Convention	Entry into force	No. of parties	Individual right to complain	State complaint	Reporting requirement	Right of investigation
African Charter on Human and Peoples' Rights	1986	54	Yes	Yes	Yes	Yes
African Charter on the Rights and Welfare of the Child	1999	49	Yes	Yes	Yes	Yes
American Convention on Human rights	1978	24	Yes	Yes	Yes	Upon complaint
Arab Charter on Human Rights	2008		No	No	Yes	No
European Convention on Human Rights and Fundamental Freedoms	1953	47	Yes	Yes	No	No
European Social Charter	1965	27	No	No	Yes	No
European Social Charter (Revised)	1999	36	No*	No	Yes	No

*Certain organisations can bring a collective complaint

Chapter XVII

International criminal law

104 Development and character of international criminal law

The foundations of international criminal law were laid after the Second World War in the indictments of leaders and soldiers from Nazi Germany, soldiers from Japan, and the Nuremberg and Tokyo trials. After 1990 the conflicts in Yugoslavia and Rwanda led to the establishment of the Yugoslavia Tribunal and the Rwanda Tribunal, as well as the conception of *international crimes*.

The four international crimes (see section 105) form the core of international criminal law in the narrow sense and can be found in particular in:

- the Rome Statute of the International Criminal Court 1998;
- other core legal texts of the International Criminal Court;
- the case law of various international criminal tribunals and national courts; and

- The Hague and Geneva Conventions on the Humanitarian Law of War.

In addition to these international crimes based on the law of war, there are a number of so-called *serious crimes* under international law, which grant states universal jurisdiction or lead to treaty-based cooperation in areas such as terrorism or transnational crimes.

105 International criminal responsibility

Individuals can be held criminally liable under international law for the following reasons:
- *International crimes* (Rome Statute of the International Criminal Court 1998):
  - □ genocide: acts committed with the intent to destroy, in whole or in part, a national, ethnic or religious group or a racial group (Article 6);
  - □ crimes against humanity: widespread or systematic attack on the civilian population with knowledge of such attack (Article 7);
  - □ war crimes: acts against persons or property protected under the provisions of the relevant Geneva Convention (Article 8);
  - □ aggression: the use of armed force by a state against the sovereignty, territorial integrity, or political independence of another state, or in any other manner inconsistent with the Charter of the United Nations (Article 8).

- *Serious crimes* (UN Convention against Transnational Organized Crime 2000):
  - □ participation in a criminal organisation (Article 5);
  - □ money laundering (Article 6);
  - □ corruption (Article 9);
  - □ trafficking in human beings (Additional Protocol 2000);
  - □ illegal production and trade in firearms (Additional Protocol 2000).
- *Special international crimes*:
  - □ piracy (Article 101 UNCLOS);
  - □ torture (Article 5 UNCAT);
  - □ terrorism (see section 112).

106 Prosecution and punishment of international crimes by national authorities

A large number of these crimes are included in national criminal law, on the basis of which national courts exercise jurisdiction under the principle of universality, regardless of by whom and where the crimes were committed.

Many states have, on the basis of bilateral and multilateral treaty obligations, both the right and the duty to prosecute and punish international crimes. In the case of international crimes, states are expected to surrender the accused to an international tribunal if they are unable or unwilling to prosecute (see section 42).

UK

The *Pinochet case* (see section 46). A Spanish extradition request for General Pinochet, the former head of state of Chile, was granted by the highest court in the UK on the basis of the UNCAT (see section 100) that had come into force for the UK in 1988.

107 International crimes in domestic criminal law

States can prosecute foreign nationals for international crimes that are committed neither in their territory nor against a citizen or vital security interest of that state (see section 105). In order to operationalise their rights and duties under general criminal international law, many states have adopted specific national legislation.

UK

In the UK, the International Criminal Court Act 2001 grants domestic jurisdiction regarding a range of international criminal acts. The Act makes it an offence 'for a person to commit genocide, a crime against humanity or a war crime' (s.51.1) and applies to acts committed in England and Wales (s.51.2.a) or acts committed 'outside the United Kingdom by a United Kingdom national, a United Kingdom resident or a person subject to UK service jurisdiction' (s.51.2.b).

In 2006 a British soldier Corporal Donald Payne became the first British person to be convicted of a war crime under this act.

108 International criminal courts and tribunals

After the Second World War several international criminal courts were established:

- The International Military Tribunal (Nuremberg Tribunal) (1945–1946) and the International Military Tribunal for the Far East (Tokyo Tribunal) (1946–1948) were created to try German and Japanese political and military leaders for war crimes. These tribunals were established by the victors of the Second World War.
- The International Criminal Tribunal for the former Yugoslavia (1997–2017), the International Criminal Tribunal for Rwanda (1994–2015), and the Special Tribunal for Lebanon (2007) were established on the basis of UNSC resolutions.
- The ICC (2002) (see section 109) was established on the basis of the Treaty of Rome and is the only tribunal of a permanent nature.

- The Special Court for Sierra Leone (2002–2013) was established by treaty between the UN and Sierra Leone.
- The Cambodia Tribunal (the Extraordinary Chambers in the Courts of Cambodia) (2006) is not formally an international tribunal but an internationalised one, in that it includes foreign judges.
- The Kosovo Specialist Chambers and Specialist Prosecutor's Office (2017) was established under Kosovan law, but seated in The Hague, and consists of international judges.

109 The International Criminal Court

The ICC's powers, jurisdiction, and modus operandi are based on:
- its Statute (Rome 1998), which entered into force in 2002;
- specific amendments to the Statute; and
- documents and resolutions concerning rules and procedures.

The ICC can exercise jurisdiction over individuals (Article 13 ICC Statute) if:
- a state party to the Statute refers a 'situation': Uganda, the Democratic Republic of Congo, the Central African Republic, and Mali, among others, have done so;

- the UNSC refers a 'situation': this has happened with Darfur, Sudan, and Libya; or
- the prosecutor 'has opened an investigation': the situations in Kenya (2009), Georgia (2016), and Burundi (2017) have prompted this.

The ICC's jurisdiction is complementary to the jurisdiction of states (Preamble and Article 1 ICC Statute), that is the ICC has jurisdiction only if the states concerned are 'unwilling or unable to conduct the prosecution' (Article 15 ICC Statute).

Several indictments have been issued against persons from the countries mentioned above since 2002. Thomas Lubanga Dyilo was the first person to be sentenced to 14 years in prison in 2012 for recruiting and assembling child soldiers, which is a war crime.

110 ICC procedure

The procedure for bringing a complaint to the ICC is shown in Figure 5.

International criminal law

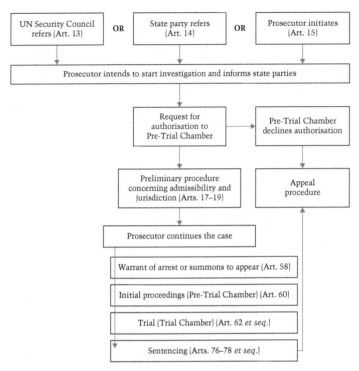

Figure 5 ICC procedure

UK

The UK is a state party to the ICC Statute and has accepted all amendments.

111 Cross-border organised crime

The increase in cross-border organised crime has led to further international cooperation between states. This cooperation is characterised by:

- an increase in the number of multilateral and bilateral treaties in the field of research and legal assistance;
- the criminalisation of serious and special crimes and the granting of specific jurisdiction; and
- the increasing activity of organisations such as INTERPOL and the UN Office on Drugs and Crime (UNODC).

The UN Convention against Transnational Organized Crime (2000) aims to combat serious crimes that have an inherent transnational component and involve an organised criminal association (Article 3.1.b). The Convention aims to promote cooperation in combating these crimes through, amongst other mechanisms:

- extradition (Article 16);
- mutual legal assistance (Article 18); and
- joint investigation (Article 19).

A criminal offence is inherently transnational when (Article 3(2)):

- it is committed in more than one state;
- it is committed in one state but a substantial part of its preparation; planning, direction, or control takes place in another state;

- it is committed in one state but involves a criminal organisation that engages in criminal activities in more than one state; or
- it is committed in one state but has substantial effects in another state.

112 Terrorism

There is no single definition of terrorism in international law. Terrorism is not qualified as an international crime and does not automatically lead to universal jurisdiction for states. International counterterrorism is governed by 19 different conventions, which form the legal framework at the international level. Most conventions regulate, among other things, the protection of civil aviation and maritime traffic and are mainly aimed at combating hijacking and hostage-taking. The following conventions focus explicitly on combating terrorism:

- The Convention on the Suppression of Terrorist Bombings (1997);
- The International Convention for the Suppression of the Financing of Terrorism (1999); and
- The Convention for the Suppression of Acts of Nuclear Terrorism (2005).

In addition to these conventions, the UN has adopted a number of binding and non-binding decisions:

- The UNGA adopted a Global Counter-Terrorism Strategy (Res. 60/288, 2006).

- The UNSC has issued a large number of binding and non-binding resolutions:
  - □ On the basis of Resolution 1267 (1999), the UNSC has established a Sanctions Committee which supervises the implementation of UNSC sanctions against individuals and organisations. The Sanctions Committee maintains a list of individuals and organisations involved in terrorist activities.
  - □ Under UNSC Resolution 1373 (2001) funds, financial assets, or economic resources may be frozen.
  - □ UNSC Resolution 2178 (2014) prohibits states and organisations from using so-called foreign fighters.

113 International organisations for combating crime

Two important international organisations have been established for the purposes of combating crime.

United Nations Office for Drugs and Crime

UNODC was established in 1997 and is based in Vienna, Austria. It assists states in combating crimes such as trafficking in human beings, drug trafficking, trafficking in protected species, money laundering, corruption, maritime crimes and piracy, terrorism, and organised crime. Its mandate extends to:
- technical cooperation and capacity-building;
- research and analysis; and
- developing treaties and promoting ratifications.

International Criminal Police Organization

INTERPOL's origins can be found in the International Police Commission, which was founded in 1923. In 1956 this NGO was turned into an IGO by giving it a treaty base (constitution). INTERPOL has its headquarters in Lyon, France. INTERPOL's constitution, titled 'Constitution of the International Criminal Police Organization–Interpol' (1956) outlines its objectives:

- promoting and facilitating cooperation between police and authorities (Article 2.1); and
- preventing and combating 'ordinary' crimes (Article 2.2).

In addition to a General Assembly, an Executive Council, and a Secretariat, INTERPOL also has National Central Offices in each Member State (Articles 31–33).

Chapter XVIII

International economic law

114 The development of international economic law

International economic law developed after 1945 on the basis of an increasing number of regional and global treaties and organisations. Economic growth was paramount until 1970. After that, international economic law started to pay attention to the consequences of free trade and economic growth on development and the environment (see also Chapter XIX).

The core of current international economic law consists of:

- international commercial law;
- international monetary law; and
- international investment law.

115 The World Trade Organization

The WTO was established in 1994 and has a threefold mission:

1. to administer a number of different multilateral trade agreements covering, inter alia, 'trade and tariffs' (the GATT Treaty), 'trade in services' (the Agreement on Trade-Related Aspects of Intellectual Property Rights (TRIPS) Treaty 1994), intellectual property, and agricultural products;
2. to facilitate trade relations and policies, including the negotiation of trade liberalization; and
3. to settle international trade disputes (see section 58).

The main bodies within the WTO are as follows:
- The Ministerial Conference is the main decision-making body. All WTO members meet there once every two years.
- The General Council is the main body for day-to-day decision-making. It has its seat in Geneva and consists of representatives of all Member States.
- The Secretariat supports and assists the various bodies.
- The DSB (see section 58).

The WTO takes decisions by consensus (see section 75).

116 The International Agreement on Tariffs and Trade

The GATT came into force in 1947 and is now – in a modified form (GATT 1994) – an integral part of the WTO.

The principles contained in the GATT form the core of international trade law:

- The most favoured nation principle. On this basis, the conditions in the most favourable agreement with one state also apply to all other states (Article I GATT 1947).
- The principle of non-discrimination prohibits states from discriminating between different trading partners and between domestic and foreign products (Article III GATT 1947).
- The principle of market access. This principle is further elaborated in the prohibition of quantitative and qualitative restrictions (Articles XI and XIII GATT 1947).

Further liberalisation of world trade is agreed after so-called trade rounds. The first five rounds focused on tariffs and lasted one year each. Since 1964 the trade rounds have lasted five years on average and the number of subjects and participants has increased fivefold. The last trade round (the Doha Round) began in 2001 and was concluded in 2006 without any significant success.

117 International monetary organisations

The most important international monetary organisations are the IMF and the World Bank Group.

Decisions within the IMF and the World Bank are made on the basis of weighted voting, that is the number of votes per state is determined by the level of that state's financial contribution to these organisations.

The objectives of the IMF are:
- stable exchange rates;
- convertibility of currency; and
- counteracting balance of payments problems.

The World Bank Group consists of:
- the International Bank for Reconstruction and Development (IBRD);
- the International Development Association (IDA); and
- the International Finance Corporation (IFC).

UK

The UK has a 4.24% share in the IMF, 4% in the IBRD, and 12.07% in the IDA.

These organisations focus on providing loans for the social, economic, and administrative development of countries. Each organisation has its own conditions.

118 Regional economic organisations and agreements

In addition to the above-mentioned global organisations, many states are also members of one or more regional economic organisations and/or agreements. These organisations generally try to promote regional economic integration by making policy agreements in one or more trade areas. The best-known regional initiatives are:

- NAFTA, which was concluded in 1994 by Canada, Mexico, and the USA to promote mutual trade and investment. The main topics are: goods, services, intellectual property, and procurement. NAFTA has its own dispute settlement regime.
- ECOWAS, which was established in 1975 to promote economic integration (Article 2 of the Treaty of Lagos). Since 2003 ECOWAS has also been involved in peacekeeping operations in Africa.
- The Benelux Union was established in 1958 by Belgium, the Netherlands, and Luxembourg as an economic union. Benelux has its own parliament, secretariat, and court of justice. Due to the success of the EU the importance of Benelux has decreased. It now mainly focuses on trademark law and the law on designs.

119 Development cooperation

After the Second World War, socio-economic and monetary cooperation focused mainly on the reconstruction of the countries destroyed by the war. As a result of the decolonisation process, socio-economic and monetary cooperation has now taken on a strongly development-oriented character.

The recognition of the right to development has been reflected in a number of specific organisations and principles:

- In the WTO it is recognised that developing countries may receive preferential treatment – the so-called *enabling clause*.
- Monetary organisations, such as the IDA, can provide loans with low interest rates.
- The UN Conference on Trade and Development (UNCTAD) and the UNDP are UN initiatives that seek to promote international cooperation in development.
- In 2000 the UNGA adopted a declaration on the Millennium Development Goals (MDGs), which set out eight development-specific goals to be achieved by 2015. Progress was reported annually. In 2015 the MDGs were replaced by the Sustainable Development Goals (SDGs) (see section 122).

Chapter XIX

International environmental law

120 The internationalisation of environmental law

The recognition of the existence of a general cross-border environmental problem has led to an internationalisation of environmental law. International environmental law is characterised by:

- an increasing recognition of environmental law principles at the international level and the recognition that environmental protection is closely linked to socio-economic and cultural developments; and
- a fragmented development reflected, inter alia, in the large number of environmental treaties and the institutionalisation of environmental law and policy (see sections 122 and 124).

121 Principles of environmental law

UN conferences, international environmental conventions, and case law have promoted and further developed the recognition of specific environmental law principles at the international level. The most important principles are as follows:

- The *principle of sic utere tuo ut alienum non laedas* (use your own in such a way that you do not harm another). In 1937, on the basis of this principle, Canada was already held liable by an arbitral tribunal for the damage suffered by American grain farmers as a result of sulphur dioxide emissions from Canadian blast furnaces (*Trail Smelter case*, Canada/USA, 1937).
- The *principle of sustainable development*. Development can be considered sustainable if:
  - □ social, economic, cultural and environmental development are in balance; and
  - □ this development is not at the expense of future generations.
- The 'polluter pays' principle provides that the costs of environmental damage, as well as the costs of preventing, reducing, and controlling environmental damage, are borne by the polluter (see e.g. Article 2(b) Convention for the Protection of the Marine Environment of the North-East Atlantic (OSPAR) 1992).
- The precautionary principle implies that preventive action should be taken to avoid environmental damage if there is a reasonable suspicion that it will occur (see, for example, Article 2(a) OSPAR).

122 UN conferences

The following three UN conferences have been important for the development of international environmental law:

- The UN Conference on the Human Environment
  (Stockholm, 1972). At the Stockholm Conference,
  the Stockholm Declaration was adopted. It contains
  25 environmental principles. This conference led
  to the establishment of UNEP (see section 123) and
  the conclusion of several environmental treaties (see
  section 124).
- The UN Conference on Environment and
  Development (Rio de Janeiro, 1992). The Rio
  Conference led to:
  □ the adoption of a declaration on environment and
     development, together with a declaration on for-
     est conservation and management;
  □ the drawing up of an international action plan,
     called Agenda 21;
  □ the signing of the Climate Convention and the
     Convention on Biodiversity; and
  □ the international recognition of the principle of
     'sustainable development'.
- The World Summit on Sustainable Development
  (Johannesburg, 2002). The main outcome of the
  Johannesburg meeting was the adoption of a declaration reaffirming the Stockholm and Rio achieve-
  ments and the adoption of a plan of implementation

for an accelerated and improved implementation of the Rio Conference goals.

- The UN Conference on Sustainable Development (Rio de Janeiro, 2012). During the conference a final document was adopted – The Future We Want – but the conference did not result in any new treaties or agreements.
- The UN Summit on Sustainable Development (New York, 2015) led to the adoption of 17 SDGs. These goals are to be achieved by 2030.

123 Institutionalisation

In institutional terms, increasing international environmental cooperation has led to the establishment of new organisations or new committees within existing organisations. The most important are:

- UNEP, which was established in 1972 on the basis of an UNGA resolution (see section 83). The organisation aims at developing an international consensus in the field of environmental protection, including the drafting of environmental treaties.
- Global Environment Facility (GEF), which was established in 1991 by the World Bank, UNEP, and UNDP. GEF provides funding for environmental projects in developing countries. It has its own secretariat.
- The WTO Committee on Trade and Environment (WTO-CTE), which was created in 1994 to facilitate the debate on the relationship between the environment and trade. All WTO members participate in

the WTO-CTE. During the Doha Round (see section 116), the WTO-CTE acted as a discussion forum for environment and development-related aspects of the negotiations.

124 Environmental treaties

International environmental regulations are contained in many different treaties. Consequently, there is a certain fragmentation in international environmental law. The main areas of interest are:
- Plant and animal protection:
  □ conventions for the protection of specific species, such as seals (Bonn, 1988) and whales (Washington, 1946);
  □ general conventions for the protection of endangered species (Washington, 1973), migratory species (Bonn, 1979), and biodiversity (Rio, 1992);
  □ conventions for the protection of specific areas, such as the Convention on Wetlands of International Importance (Ramsar, 1971).
- Climate change and ozone layer protection: Climate Convention (Rio, 1992), Kyoto Protocol (Kyoto, 1997), and the Paris Agreement (2015).
- Water and soil protection: the Desertification Convention (Paris, 1994) and the various conventions for the protection of rivers, lakes, and seas, such as the Rhine Convention (Berne, 1963) and the Convention for the Prevention of Pollution from Ships (London, 1973).

List of consulted literature

Crawford, J. *Brownlie's Principles of Public International Law* (9th ed., Oxford University Press, 2019)

Hernández, G. *International Law* (Oxford University Press, 2019)

Klabbers, J. *International Law* (3rd ed., Cambridge University Press, 2020)

Mansell, W. and Openshaw, K. *International Law: A Critical Introduction* (2nd ed., Hart, 2019)

Shaw, M. *International Law* (9th ed., Oxford University Press, 2021)

Wallace, R. and Martin-Ortega, O. *International Law* (9th ed., Sweet & Maxwell, 2020)

Index

Index

Index

Index